OUTBACK EVANGELIST

THE STORY OF ERNEST AND EUPHEMIA KRAMER

ELVA SCHROEDER

WITH

FAITH KRAMER METTERS

Even Before Publishing
www.evenbeforepublishing.com

Outback Evangelist: The Story of Ernest and Euphemia Kramer
Published by Even Before Publishing, a division of Wombat Books
P. O. Box 1519, Capalaba Qld 4157
www.evenbeforepublishing.com
www.wombatbooks.com.au

© Elva Schroeder and Faith Kramer Metters 2011
Design and layout by Even Before Publishing

ISBN: 978-1-921633-69-0
Previously published by Peacock Publications ISBN: 1921008881
September 2008

National Library of Australia Cataloguing-in-Publication entry
Author: Schroeder, Elva
Title: Outback evangelist: the story of Ernest and Euphemia
         Kramer/ Elva Schroeder with Faith Kramer Metters
Edition: 2nd
ISBN: 9781921633690 (pbk.)
Subjects: Kramer, Ernest E. (Ernest Eugene), 1889-1958.
         Kramer, Euphemia, 1887-1971.
         Missionaries--South Australia--Biography.
         Aboriginal Australians--Missions--South Australia.
Other Authors/Contributors:
         Metters, Faith Kramer.
Dewey Number: 266.0092

All rights reserved. No part of this publication may be reproduced, stored in, or introduced into a retrieval system, or transmitted, in any form, or by any means (electronic, mechanical, photocopying, recording or otherwise) without the prior written permission of the publisher.

Note: It is both illegal and a violation of Christian ethics to copy any of this material without permission in writing from the publisher.

DEDICATED TO

The memory of my parents,

Ernest and Euphemia Kramer,

brother Colin

and

sisters Mary and Grace

Other Books by Elva Schroeder

Whatever Happened to the Twelve Apostles?

Doctor Sahib : The story of Doctor Cecil Mead

Cathy : A Romance set in Papua New Guinea

Secret Cavern : for readers 8-12 years

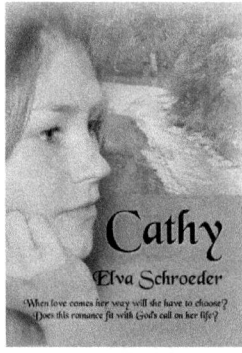

To purchase copies of this book contact
Elva Schroeder
Phone (08) 8387 1197
Email : jimelva@ozemail.com.au

OR

Faith Kramer Metters
Phone : (08) 8276 8606
Email : hfmetters@aandr.com.au

OR

Your local Christian bookstore.

ACKNOWLEDGMENTS

I would like to express my appreciation for the efforts of my dear sister, Mary, who is now enjoying the glories of heaven in the presence of her Saviour.

Over the years Mary collected newspaper cuttings, diaries, and other materials relating to the outback ministry of our parents, Ernest and Euphemia Kramer.

Before she died, Mary passed on to me the task of putting this all together that God might be glorified through the story of their lives and ministry, and daily proving of His keeping power.

However, I eventually passed on the task of writing their story to my friend, Elva Schroeder, and the book you now have is the result of her work on our behalf.

Faith Kramer Metters

'God has chosen the foolish things of the world to put to shame the wise, and God has chosen the weak things of the world to put to shame the things which are mighty.'
1 Corinthians 1:27

*Euphemia and Ernest Kramer on their
35th Wedding Anniversary, 21st March 1947*

Contents

ACKNOWLEDGMENTS		5
Chapter 1	KRAMER MEMORIAL CHURCH	11
Chapter 2	THE WEAKLING	13
Chapter 3	EUPHEMIA BUCHANAN	17
Chapter 4	WHEREVER GOD LEADS	22
Chapter 5	GOING NORTH	26
Chapter 6	SECOND TRIP NORTH	34
Chapter 7	FARINA TO OODNADATTA	40
Chapter 8	THIRD TRIP NORTH	45
Chapter 9	ALICE SPRINGS	52
Chapter 10	HERMANNSBURG	56
Chapter 11	A NEW VISION	60
Chapter 12	TRIALS AND BLESSINGS	65
Chapter 13	A NEW HOME	70
Chapter 14	CAMEL TREKKING	76
Chapter 15	NEW BEGINNINGS	81
Chapter 16	CHANGES	85
Chapter 17	DEVELOPMENTS	88
Chapter 18	FAR AND WIDE	95
Chapter 19	END OF THE ROAD	102
Chapter 20	AFTERWARDS	109
Appendix: Letter from Governor Sir Douglas Nicholls		114
Mortock Library Papers - 1		115
Mortock Library Papers - 2		116

Kramer Memorial Church in Alice Springs

Chapter 1

KRAMER MEMORIAL CHURCH

It was a beautiful autumn day in Alice Springs, Easter Saturday, the 9th April 1977. A large crowd had gathered in Parke Crescent for the opening of the Kramer Memorial Church erected by the Australian Missionary Society in memory of Ernest Kramer, pioneer missionary to Central Australia.

This interdenominational church for white, half-caste and Aboriginal people, had taken nine years to complete, using volunteer labour and gifts, but was now being opened debt free. It was the first work undertaken by Mobile Mission Maintenance, a group of Christian tradesmen from three states, who gave their services voluntarily. The secretary of the group, Mr David Dawson of Melbourne, was invited to officially open the church.

Among those present were Mr Kramer's four adult children, Colin, Mary, Faith and Grace, along with Colin's wife, Phyllis, and Grace's husband, Douglas Dawson. Miss Mary Kramer spoke on behalf of the Aborigines' Friends' Association with which her father had long been associated. She said it was her prayer that many people would come to know the Lord Jesus Christ as their own personal Saviour within those walls. That it would be a place where Aboriginal people could worship God with no denominational or racial pressures. She then unveiled a portrait of Ernest Kramer to be hung in the church.

Greetings were received from around Australia, including a letter from the Governor of South Australia, Sir Douglas Nicholls, who wrote to Mary, 'Your father's name was widely respected for the great work he did as a missionary and we are delighted to know that his successor has seen fit to arrange for this new church to be dedicated in memory of your father.'

Mr Arnold Long, missioner in Alice Springs, whose vision it was to build the church, said he counted Ernest Kramer as a valued personal friend. He went on, 'It has been our experience over the years in the inland to meet hundreds of Indigenous folk who knew God's servant in the days when, with wonderful faith and energy, he penetrated great areas with the gospel message and with practical help for the hungry, the sick and the dying.

'We know of nobody who more effectively captured the love and loyalty of the people to whom he ministered. They looked to him as a father. Furthermore we have no doubt that a great many will be among the redeemed multitudes in heaven because of his going out among them.

'Even now, forty-two years since God's servants left Alice Springs, there are many of the older Indigenous folk scattered over the country who arise to bless their name and who have learned to love that Name which is above every name because these servants of the Lord ventured forth at His command.'

One of the many Aboriginal folk present at the opening service said Mr Kramer was the best friend he had ever known.

Among Ernest Kramer's other friends in Central Australia were the Reverend John Flynn of the Flying Doctor Service, Dr Charles Duguid, founder of the Ernabella Aboriginal Mission, Anthropologists Professor John Cleland and Professor Ted Strehlow, son of Pastor Carl Strehlow, and Lutheran Pastor Frederich Albrecht of the Hermannsburg Mission.

So just who was Ernest Kramer and how did he, with his wife Effie, come to spend twenty-one years traversing the harsh, inhospitable territory of Central Australia with the redeeming message of God's love and forgiveness for all who would receive it?

Chapter 2

THE WEAKLING

Ernest Eugene Kramer first saw the light of day on the 10th May 1889 in Basle, Switzerland. The ninth child in his family, Erny realised early on that he was an 'unwanted child'. Serious digestion problems caused further distress with Erny unable to keep down nourishment of any kind. In her despair, his mother summoned their pastor to christen Erny, to make sure he didn't pass away without a name. His struggle for existence was eventually aided by beaten egg whites which helped put a lining on his stomach.

School was a constant challenge for Erny, who was always weak and sickly, and unable to join in sports or games of any kind.

Erny's mother was a woman of prayer and the Bible. From her example he was inspired to search out spiritual values. At school Erny loved the weekly two hour Bible lessons and many of the stories he heard then stayed with him throughout his life. He also read some deeply spiritual books belonging to his mother's father. Erny longed to possess the victorious spiritual life he read about in the books, but as soon as he thought he was getting closer he found evil triumphing within him, and he would be filled with remorse and discouragement.

When Erny was eleven he attended a Salvation Army meeting and joyfully gave his life to the Lord. But when his father found out, he forbade Erny to have anything more to do with them.

Erny was only fourteen when, on the 15th December 1903, his mother passed to her heavenly reward and he felt her passing keenly. She left behind a letter in which she expressed her confidence that the Spirit of Christ would guide all her children, and urged them to to follow His calling. To Erny, in death, his mother's face revealed that 'Peace like a river', of which she had so often sung.

When Erny was sixteen he was confirmed and received at the Communion of the Swiss Protestant State Church. But there was still a deep dissatisfaction and longing in his heart for something more. Around this time Erny was greatly influenced by an old philosopher with whom he took long walks. His brother, Carl, also told him about some of the cults of India and Erny looked into anything he felt would help him find meaning and purpose in life. In an effort to improve himself he studied philosophy and tried various diets and exercises.

Eventually Erny received a diploma from the Worms Milling Academy and succeeded in holding down an accreditable position in a newly established, up-to-date Flour Mill, having passed through its technical workings and office management. But deep down in his heart there was still an unsatisfied craving for God.

While walking along the banks of the River Rhine on the fifth anniversary of his mother's death in December 1908, an unknown inner Voice gave him a presentiment that he would go to a far off land and he said to himself, 'Where?'

His ill health persisted and when Erny was twenty his doctor advised him to leave the mill and spend time at a sanatorium in the Alps to recuperate. When bidding farewell to the firm's director, Erny mentioned that he feared he would not return. The boss, a shrewd businessman, said with a tear in his eye, 'You will have spoilt your career if you do not return – a post by my side stands open to you!'

A few weeks after his return to Basle from the Alps, Erny heard a lecture on Australia by an Australian doctor who specialised in herbal remedies. As the man spoke, suddenly it seemed like an arrow to Erny's soul with the firm conviction – TO AUSTRALIA I MUST GO!

The doctor and his wife agreed to accompany Erny as interpreter and guide, and as if by a miracle his father was also willing to let him go. Seven weeks after the lecture, on the 24th July 1909, they left Basle on the *Suevie* via London, Bristol and Liverpool for Australia. Erny, however, was a very poor sailor and spent much of the voyage extremely seasick. He was most relieved when the coast of Australia finally appeared on the horizon.

Originally the doctor had planned to land in Albany, but at the last minute he changed his mind and they proceeded on to Adelaide, landing at Outer Harbor on the 9th September 1909. However, the doctor turned out to be a con man who relieved Erny of his return fare to Basle, Switzerland, then shot through, leaving Erny stranded in a strange land without money, no understanding of the country or its culture, and very little knowledge of English.

A kindly Methodist minister and his wife took Erny into their home. With their help, and by diligent study of his German-English Bible, Erny gradually managed to grasp enough of the language to find his way around. But for twenty-year-old Erny that first summer was a real challenge. The unaccustomed heat and dryness did not agree with him and his health suffered.

With his limited knowledge of English, and having his Diploma and other papers in German, Erny had to start working at the bottom of the ladder again in a small galvanised iron mill. After six months he collapsed and was stricken with severe inflammation of the bowel. For twenty-one days he could not eat anything and just drank lemon or pineapple juice. Throughout this time he was patiently cared for by the Methodist minister's wife.

During his weakest moments Erny felt the voice of Jesus calling him to full surrender. Even though he could not speak, he gladly yielded and his heart said, 'I am saved to serve!' Prayer had been offered for him by his brother Fred and his friends in California and slowly Erny recovered. At first he had to walk with the aid of a broom but gradually his strength returned. Erny spent much of this time studying his German-English Bible, mainly to improve his understanding of English, but at the same time God's word, in both languages, was being deeply embedded in his heart and mind.

Eventually Erny was able to look for work again but not in the mill. He got a job painting fences, but being a perfectionist, he was too slow and this did not pay. Finally, he took a position as a travelling salesman, but before long his conscience smote him over the quality of the goods he was asked to sell.

One day, feeling quite hopeless and desperately forsaken, Erny was strongly tempted to end his misery and loneliness in the ocean, but God, in His mercy, prevented him from doing so. Returning to the city Erny found a letter from his brother, Fred, a dedicated Christian, saying he was on his way from California to Australia.

When Fred arrived he urged Erny to surrender his will completely to the Lord. After a brief struggle, Erny did so and a great joy welled up in his heart at the assurance that through the blood of Christ alone he was now a child of God. On a Sunday morning in February 1911, he was joyously baptised by Fred in the River Torrens close to the Adelaide Zoo. Soon afterwards Erny accompanied Fred to a nearby park and in halting English he testified to the new life and joy he had found in Christ.

With a new hunger in his heart for the things of God, Erny and Fred found fellowship with a little group of Christians who met in an upper room. Here Erny felt himself filled with a deep spirit of prayer and longing for God. Many times he experienced gracious anointings of the Spirit of God, yet still he yearned for more of God in his life.

Eventually Fred felt they should move on to Melbourne, and together they set out on their push bikes for the 454 mile (727 km) trip. They arrived on the 28th April 1911 and went straight to a service at a little Gospel Hall loosely connected with the one they had attended in Adelaide. Afterwards they were able to obtain accommodation in a small room at the back of the mission. For three days the brothers attended prayer times in this little hall, with Erny on his face before God, seeking the outpouring of His Spirit in his life.

Finally, on the 1st May, as Erny was lost in praise and thanksgiving to God, he felt floods of overflowing joy fill his whole being, like the streams of living water promised by Jesus in John 7:37-38. He had never before known such joy or wonder in his innermost being. Like a spring of water the power of the Holy Spirit bubbled up within him and overflowed until his whole body and soul felt aglow with the ecstasy and joy of God's presence.

Five days after Erny's arrival in Melbourne and two days after his overwhelming experience of God's love, Erny met a Mrs Buchanan who had come to the mission from her farm in South Gippsland seeking more of God. She was accompanied by her third daughter, Euphemia. Little did Erny realise at the time that Mrs Buchanan was to become a loving mother to him and that Euphemia was to play such an important role in his life and work for God.

Chapter 3

EUPHEMIA BUCHANAN

Euphemia Buchanan was born on the 18th July 1886 in the small country town of Creswick, north of Ballarat, Victoria, the third daughter in a family of five girls and two boys. Her four grandparents came from Scotland, but both her parents were born in Australia. The family moved to a dairy farm at Bena, in South Gippsland, Victoria, when Effie, as she was called, was nine months old. But when Effie was twelve months old she became very ill and for three months she had to be carried on a pillow. Her sister, Kit, who was nineteen months younger than Effie, walked before she did.

Effie was always tiny and not very strong and missed much of her early schooling through illness. She finished school with anything but a good education. However, she loved Sunday School and from a very early age Effie had a longing to be a missionary and take the gospel to those who had never heard. She would cut out missionary pictures and stories and paste them in a book. Effie loved to read their reports of how they had received their call from God and she used to think, 'Oh, if only I could go to India, China, Korea or somewhere for God.'

Eventually Effie became a Sunday School teacher herself. However, in her teens, she developed a liking for dancing, even though she knew her God-fearing parents would not approve. One night she attended a party at a friend's house and danced until 2.00am. It was pouring with rain so Effie and her two brothers had to stay the night. But once in bed, Effie tossed and turned under the conviction of the Holy Spirit. Although a Communicant in the Presbyterian Church, Effie had had no real heart change or personal experience with God to this time.

Several more dancing parties followed, then one night, as Effie watched the others whirling around the floor at 2.00am, suddenly into her mind came the words, 'Whatsoever you do in word or deed do all to the glory of God.' During their walk home through wet grass around 4.00am Effie battled with this thought and promised God, 'Never again!'

Yet the flesh was weak and once more she found herself dancing the night away. But this time on her return home, Effie felt so disgusted with her own weakness, that she fell on her knees beside her bed and cried out, 'Lord, I'm helpless! I don't want to dance but I can't give it up. Please take the desire right away from me.' From that moment on she never again had the desire to dance.

Although only 4ft 9ins (145cm) tall, Effie had always been popular with the young men. In time she found herself strongly attracted to one in particular, but this ended in deep disappointment and Effie wondered if she would ever marry. Yet she found herself thinking that if she did, she would like her husband to be stronger in the Lord than she was, one who could help her keep on the upward path of life.

Effie's mother was ever seeking a closer walk with God and when she heard of a group in Melbourne who were helping people discover a deeper experience with God, she decided to visit them. Effie accompanied her and they spent one week at the mission. Effie's mother found that deeper experience with God she had been seeking, but all Effie wanted to do was explore the big city.

However, the night before they were to leave for home, Mrs Buchanan decided to be baptised by immersion. Although Effie didn't know what the scriptures said about it she decided, if her mother was going to leave the Presbyterian Church and become a Baptist, she might as well do the same. That night they were both baptised by a keen young Christian named Fred Kramer. It was the 10th May 1911, his younger brother Erny's 22nd birthday.

Effie and her mother returned home the next day, yet Effie was left with the feeling that the people in that little mission had a deep love and something else that she didn't possess. Even so, she felt no particular desire to return and discover what it was. She just wanted life to continue on as it always had, safe and secure on their South Gippsland farm.

Then suddenly her whole world was turned upside down. First, her Grandmother died, and her father and uncle went off to her funeral. Then while they were away her mother became seriously ill and she and Effie's eldest sister, Flora, were away for five weeks. All this meant Effie had to take on more work on the farm than her strength allowed. Finally her health broke, the cough that was always with her became much worse, and eventually her sisters persuaded her to return to the little mission hall in Melbourne.

Here they prayed for her healing but there was no improvement. However, Effie now found she had a much deeper problem than the need for physical healing. When she tried to join in singing, 'At the cross, at the cross where I first saw the light,' something inside her whispered, 'But you haven't seen any light.' Just then a lady beside her asked if she wanted to say a word for the Lord. Effie realised that she didn't have any thing to say, and asked the group to pray for her. They did and she felt a peace and happiness within that she had never known before.

The next evening was a special healing service so Effie again asked for prayer for healing. As they prayed for her, an older lady suddenly said, 'Effie, do you know the Lord wants you?' Effie replied that she didn't think the Lord even noticed her. She was such a stubborn, self-willed, insignificant little creature she couldn't imagine Him ever wanting her. When Effie was assured that He did, she felt deeply humbled.

That night after saying her prayers Effie got into bed. But as she lay there, she began to feel extremely happy. Suddenly she was aware of a beautiful sensation starting in the soles of her feet and working up through every part of her body until it reached her heart where it remained like a loving hand touching her heart. She breathed deeply, sensing it was the Lord. Then very quietly she began to say 'Praise God, praise God!' something she had vowed never to do. The next morning her deep happiness remained and she found herself marching easily up the stairs, singing as she went, her heart overflowing with the love of God.

Effie's time was now up to return home, but her mother wrote encouraging her to stay longer if she needed to. Effie prayed earnestly that God would make His will clear to her. Was she to go to the mission field and if so where, or should she return home and help on the farm?

Then the way was made plain for her. Two men from the mission were travelling to Gippsland to hold services. They would be staying at Effie's home and would appreciate her assistance with the meetings. The younger of the two men was Ernest Kramer. Effie's parents met them at the station and for most of the six mile (almost 10 km) trip to the farm, they joyfully sang one gospel song after another, including, 'This is my story, this is my song, praising my Saviour all the day long.'

The next day was Saturday and the two guests readily joined in helping on the farm. While working in the fields with Effie's brother, Jim, Ernest Kramer was used by God to lead him to trust in the Lord as his Saviour. This was the start of a great move of God in their family. Within a few days Erny had also led Effie's youngest brother, Alex, to the Lord. Then one after the other, Effie's four sisters, brother-in-law and several friends all came into a saving knowledge of the Lord Jesus, many weeping their way to the foot of the cross.

Day after day Effie was so filled with the joy of the Lord that she would wake first thing in the morning with a song of praise to God in her heart and on her lips. One morning she was awakened at 2.00am with a strong impression to read Isaiah 55 and she felt strongly that God was calling her to take His message to those who had not heard it. The following morning she said to her older sister, Madge, 'I don't know what the Lord has in store for me, but I don't think I am going to be home for long.' Tears streamed down Madge's face as she replied, 'I have the same feeling Eff.'

One morning soon after this, Effie read Ecclesiastes 4:9-10 – 'Two are better than one, because they have a good reward for their labor. For if they fall, one will lift up his companion.' God made this very real to Effie, and she felt He was showing her that He had a life's partner already picked out for her.

That very evening, Ernest Kramer opened his heart to her and as they talked they could clearly see the Lord's guiding hand in preparing them for each other. When they broke the news to Effie's parents, the four of them shared a blessed time of prayer as they saw God's plan in it all.

On the 21st March 1912, Ernest Kramer and Euphemia Buchanan, with Madge as bridesmaid, were joined in marriage in a joyful Christian ceremony It was a happy start to what was to be a long life of devoted service to their Lord and Saviour.

Chapter 4

WHEREVER GOD LEADS

Erny and Effie had agreed beforehand that they would go wherever God led and trust Him only to meet all their needs. Immediately after their marriage they were put in charge of a men's home where they saw many drunken lives reclaimed and learnt valuable lessons in trusting God.

On Tuesday evenings they held special prayer meetings and various friends came early in time for tea. One night Effie was expecting ten people for the evening meal and had only a small piece of fish to cook for them all. She asked God to put it into a certain person's mind to bring them fish instead of his usual gift of fruit. That person didn't even show up that night but another man arrived with a large package of fish, and told Effie how the Lord had impressed on him to buy it for her. Effie learned that night not to tell God HOW to meet their needs, but to trust Him to do whatever He knew was best.

Some time earlier Effie had had a dream that her husband went away to work amongst Aboriginal people, leaving her behind. Then the dream changed and she was walking towards Erny surrounded by Aborigines and holding a little white baby in her arms. But she quickly dismissed this as just a dream.

During their time at the men's home, they met a number of missionaries, including a lady who was working among Aborigines in New South Wales, and caring for a dear little orphaned Aboriginal girl. A short time later, at one of their weekly prayer meetings, the Lord put a deep love and yearning in Erny's heart both for the Aboriginal people and for white people in the bush who had no Christian witness and he began to seek the Lord for His will in the matter.

He shared his experience with Effie and as they spent time before the Lord, an intense longing to take the gospel to the Aboriginal people came over them both, along with the strong conviction that this was the work God was calling them to.

Shortly after this an opportunity arose in South Australia to work among Aboriginal people and they felt led to offer their services. They were accepted and looked to the Lord to guide their steps and meet every need. One morning a lady came to Effie and told her another sister in the Lord had given her money to buy anything they needed and she wanted Effie to come shopping with her. Another confirmation that God was indeed leading them into this work.

However, Effie was soon to become a mother, and it was decided that she should remain in Melbourne until after the event, which meant Erny going on ahead. At first Effie was deeply distressed about this, but after she and Erny had a special time of prayer together she was given God's wondrous peace concerning the situation.

The following Tuesday morning Effie stood with others and cheerfully waved Erny off on the boat bound for the River Murray in South Australia. Two months later, on the 28th January 1913, Effie became the proud mother of a little boy whom she named Colin Eugene after his grandfather Buchanan and Erny's second name.

When Colin was six weeks old, Effie's parents accompanied her to South Australia. As Effie walked towards Erny with Colin in her arms, she suddenly realised that her dream of eleven months previously was being fulfilled before her very eyes. God had known what was going to happen before Effie even knew she was going to be a mother!

Erny was thrilled with the little bundle of joy Effie handed him, but to Effie's amusement Erny held their baby son most gingerly, as if afraid he would break. Effie's parents stayed with them for a week but when they left Effie felt so weak she wondered how she was going to manage to care for her little baby and work for the Lord as well.

In answer to prayer Effie's strength gradually returned and before long she was able to accompany Erny as he carried a thriving baby Colin from camp to camp along the River Murray to share the good news of Jesus with the Aboriginal community. The Aboriginal women loved to hold the little white baby and claimed he was their own little missionary.

Erny first worked among a small group of Aborigines and half-castes at a place called Manuka near Mannum on the River Murray. The Aborigines here were used to receiving government rations and handouts which they quickly spent on drinking and gambling, and they didn't take readily to Erny's suggestions that their lives would be better spent working to support themselves.

After Effie's arrival, a man who owned property nearby offered Erny half an acre of his land and furnished a small shack for them to live in. He also sold them a cow which was just coming into milk. This seemed an ideal proposition, with Colin soon needing milk to drink, and all seemed to be going well. However, they became concerned when the man said he wanted them to teach the Aborigines to work for him. Then one morning they awoke to find all the Aborigines had left and gone further up river. To continue to help them Erny and Effie needed to follow.

That morning in their devotions they were singing, 'When I was willing from all things to part, He gave me His bountiful love in my heart.' A sudden conviction seized Effie and she said, 'Oh, Erny, the Lord wants us to give that cow back and just follow where He leads us.' Erny said, 'If that is so we will go.' However, when they went over and told the man of their decision, he cursed and swore at them for spoiling all his plans.

Erny and Effie turned and walked sorrowfully back to their little hut and began packing their possessions. But now they had another problem. They were one and a half miles (over 2 kms) from the river boat landing, with no Aborigines to help them and no way to transport their possessions over there. Again they gave themselves to prayer and waited on God for the answer.

A few hours later, their landlord appeared, but he was calm and friendly now. He invited them to his home for the evening meal and said his son would afterwards come with the horse and dray and take their possessions over to the boat landing. Into Effie's mind came the verse, 'When a man's ways please the Lord he makes even his enemies to be at peace with him.'

It was a perfect starry night, and as they walked beside the dray Erny said, 'Tonight we are just like the Lord Jesus, with nowhere to lay our heads and no money even to pay our passage on the boat.' It was midnight when the boat arrived and after hearing Erny's story, the kindly captain told them not to worry about anything. He showed them to a very nice cabin where they enjoyed a good night's rest until they reached the Aborigines' camp near Swan Reach around 7.00am the next morning.

The Indigenous people welcomed them cheerfully and helped carry all their possessions from the boat to their camp. The local police were also pleased to see them, feeling Erny and Effie would be a good influence on the Aborigines of the area. The Aborigines helped them build a wurley, similar to their own and, with no bed or furniture, they slept on mother earth that night. The next day, while they were out gathering dry grass to make a bed, Effie lost her wedding ring. She was distraught over this, but although they searched frantically, they were unable to find it.

There were about twelve children in the Aboriginal camp, and around this time one little girl named Olive opened her heart to the Saviour. But she was a sickly little girl, and as her condition worsened, she could be heard singing softly, 'Jesus loves me this I know'. At her funeral, Erny told the people that she had gone to be with Jesus and that they must repent and turn to Him if they wished to meet Olive again. The next morning an old lady came, shook her fist at Erny and said he was lucky he hadn't been speared the previous day as it was forbidden to mention the name of a dead person. Another lesson had been learned.

Erny often rode his bicycle to various Indigenous camps in the area to share the good news of Jesus. One day he was observed mending a puncture and singing, "The toils of the road will seem nothing when we get to the end of the way." After a few months quite a number of Aboriginal folk had responded to the Lord and were baptised. But these had all heard the gospel long before Erny and Effie arrived among them eight months earlier and they began to feel a burden on their hearts to reach out to those who had never once heard the message of God's love and forgiveness.

One old man in the camp seemed advanced enough in the Lord to take services and conduct Sunday School, so Erny and Effie began praying that God would show them where they were to move on to from there. They were in prayer one day when they both felt that the Lord was telling them they were to go to the far north where the people had never before heard the gospel.

Chapter 5

GOING NORTH

They packed their meagre belongings and returned to Adelaide, where they were welcomed by a dear old couple who had known Erny soon after he first arrived in Adelaide. It was decided that Effie and Colin would stay with a Christian family thirteen miles (21 kms) out of Adelaide, while Erny took his bicycle and travelled north on the train to check things out. This time, although Effie missed Erny terribly, she coped with the separation much better than she had twelve months previously.

Erny stayed at Port Augusta for about six weeks, and felt that would be a good place to work out from. But after travelling in various directions on his bicycle, he decided that was not the way to travel up there. They would need a caravan and some animals so they could travel from station to station to minister to both the white and Aboriginal people of each area.

During the two months Effie stayed with her new friends she received gifts amounting to eleven pounds ($22) from various sources. When she learned of Erny's plans, she used the money to buy two tents, a small camp stove and other things they would need. Then, after praying about it, she decided to use some of the money to purchase another wedding ring. The jeweller, thinking she was a new bride, gave her six silver teaspoons and a silver pin tray. The daughter of the family where she was staying was about to be married and Effie had wanted to give her a present but had no money to spare. Now she was able to give the lass the six silver teaspoons and her mother the silver pin tray as a Christmas present in appreciation for all their kindness to her and Colin.

Effie had realised she would need to buy several summer dresses to take north with her, but by the time she had completed her other purchases she found she had only one half-penny ($1/_2$c) left. However, that night the lady of the house presented Effie with six lovely cotton dresses ready for her trip north.

On his return Erny bought a greengrocer's old van and converted it to a home for Effie and Colin. He fitted it out with shelves for storage plus sleeping facilities for when it rained. Then, after painting the outside green, he used the signwriting skills he had learned from his father to add various Bible texts on the sides. These included, 'Behold I come quickly and my reward is with me to give to every man as His work shall be,' Revelation 22:12; 'Thou shalt call His name Jesus for He shall save His people from their sins,' Matthew 1:21; 'God is love', I John 4:16; and 'Prepare to meet thy God', Amos 4:12.

It was to a large extent through studying the Bible that Erny had been brought to faith in the Lord and he felt that, with no denominational backing, the one thing he could take to the people of the north was an open Bible. So he approached the British and Foreign Bible Society and was provided with a plentiful supply of Bibles, New Testaments and other literature to distribute. He also prepared a basic medical kit, both for their own needs and also to render first aid to those in need along the way.

Finally, in January 1914, Erny and Effie set out with one year old Colin to answer the call God had placed on their hearts for the people of the outback. With two sturdy horses they set out for Port Augusta via Kadina and Wallaroo. At Wallaroo they met up with Methodist minister, Reverend Sammy Forsythe, who was to become a close friend and supporter of their work.

But as they headed north, Effie soon found that just day to day living presented quite a challenge in itself. Along with coping with the extreme summer heat, preparing meals over an open fire or in the small camp stove, and doing the daily wash in a kerosene tin, she had to be ever on the alert for snakes, scorpions and other dangers as little Colin toddled around their campsite.

They eventually arrived safely at Port Augusta, where they spent some time reaching out to the Aborigines of the area, and had the joy of seeing quite a few turn to the Lord. Then, on the advice of local bushmen, they replaced their two horses with four sturdy donkeys before setting out in their van to take the gospel to those who had never heard it. Heading out along the east-west Transcontinental Railway line, then under construction, they shared the gospel and Christian literature with railway fettlers, station people and Aboriginal groups all the way through to the end of the line at Tarcoola, 251 miles (402km) north-west of Port Augusta.

The little town of Tarcoola had been set up in 1901 to service both the Tarcoola gold fields – so named in 1893 after a race horse of that name which had recently won the Melbourne Cup – and later the railway workers. Here Erny and Effie had many opportunities to share the gospel, as well as being able to stock up on needed supplies.

While at Tarcoola they heard the news of the June 28th assassination of Archduke Franz Ferdinand, heir to the Austro-Hungarian throne, which within a month had led to a state of open warfare throughout much of Europe. Erny was deeply saddened at the news, and prayed that the war would soon be over.

However, life there in outback Australia seemed a world away from the European situation and before long they packed up and moved on along the line. Eventually they reached the clearing gang about thirty miles (48km) past the Tarcoola goldfields and again found many doors open to them to share the good news of Jesus Christ with both whites and Indigenous people.

The texts on their van never failed to attract attention and many a time as their faithful donkeys slowly plodded along through the heavy sand they were greeted with humorous comments on the words, 'Behold I come quickly!' But at least, Erny consoled himself, it meant the railway workers were getting God's word one way or another.

Then in late March 1915 Effie went down with enteric fever. She became seriously ill and in her delirium feared she was dying. Erny said to her, 'No darling, you shall not die, but live.' After spending the night in prayer at her bedside, early the next morning Erny harnessed up the donkeys, made a bed in the van for Effie and carried her to it. Then, with two-year-old Colin sitting up on the seat beside him, he set off, praying fervently that God would keep them all safe.

It took two and a half days to cover the forty-five miles (72 km) back to the nearest station where Erny pitched the tent two miles from the head station, made up Effie's bed and carried her into the tent. It was 145 miles

(232 kms) to the Port Augusta Hospital and Effie could never have stood the journey. But Erny patiently cared for her and Colin, having to spoon feed Effie, and little by little, she gradually regained her strength.

It took two weeks for letters to get to Melbourne. When Effie's parents learned of her sickness, they immediately wrote asking that Effie and Colin come home as soon as she was able to travel and they would send the money for her fare, and for Erny to sell the van and come too. But Effie had recovered enough by then that, after praying about it, she felt God impressed on her the words of Psalm 11:1, 'In the Lord I put my trust. How can you say to my soul, flee as a bird to your mountain.' So she wrote and thanked them, but said they would not be coming home just yet, as they felt God still had more for them to do out there, but would endeavour to join the family for Christmas.

It was now autumn and far more pleasant for travelling. Also, they were able to buy fresh fruit, vegetables and eggs from the train which helped in Effie's recovery. Once she was well enough they moved on along the line to the 115 mile (184 km) camp where they found the enteric fever had now broken out. There were 300 men in this camp and every week more were laid low with the fever and taken to the Pt Augusta Hospital where quite a number died. They stayed at this camp for two weeks and at the open air meetings Effie stood up and witnessed to the Lord's healing touch in sparing her life.

From there they journeyed along the route of the railway line 145 miles (232 km) beyond Tarcoola. It was rough and desolate country, yet they had many wonderful opportunities to hold gospel services and witness for the Lord. The wife of one man who gladly listened told them her husband hadn't been inside a church since they were married fifteen years earlier.

At a boarding house along the line the hostess took them in rather warily, not knowing who they were or what their objective was, but before they left she asked them into her private room to have prayer with her. On leaving Effie, gave her a little pamphlet to read to her nine-year-old daughter. It was entitled, *Talks to Little Girls About Themselves*. The mother threw her arms around Effie and thanked her, saying she was so glad to find one woman who had the welfare of their girls on her heart. She pressed five shillings (50c) into Effie's hand to enable her to buy more literature to give to other women.

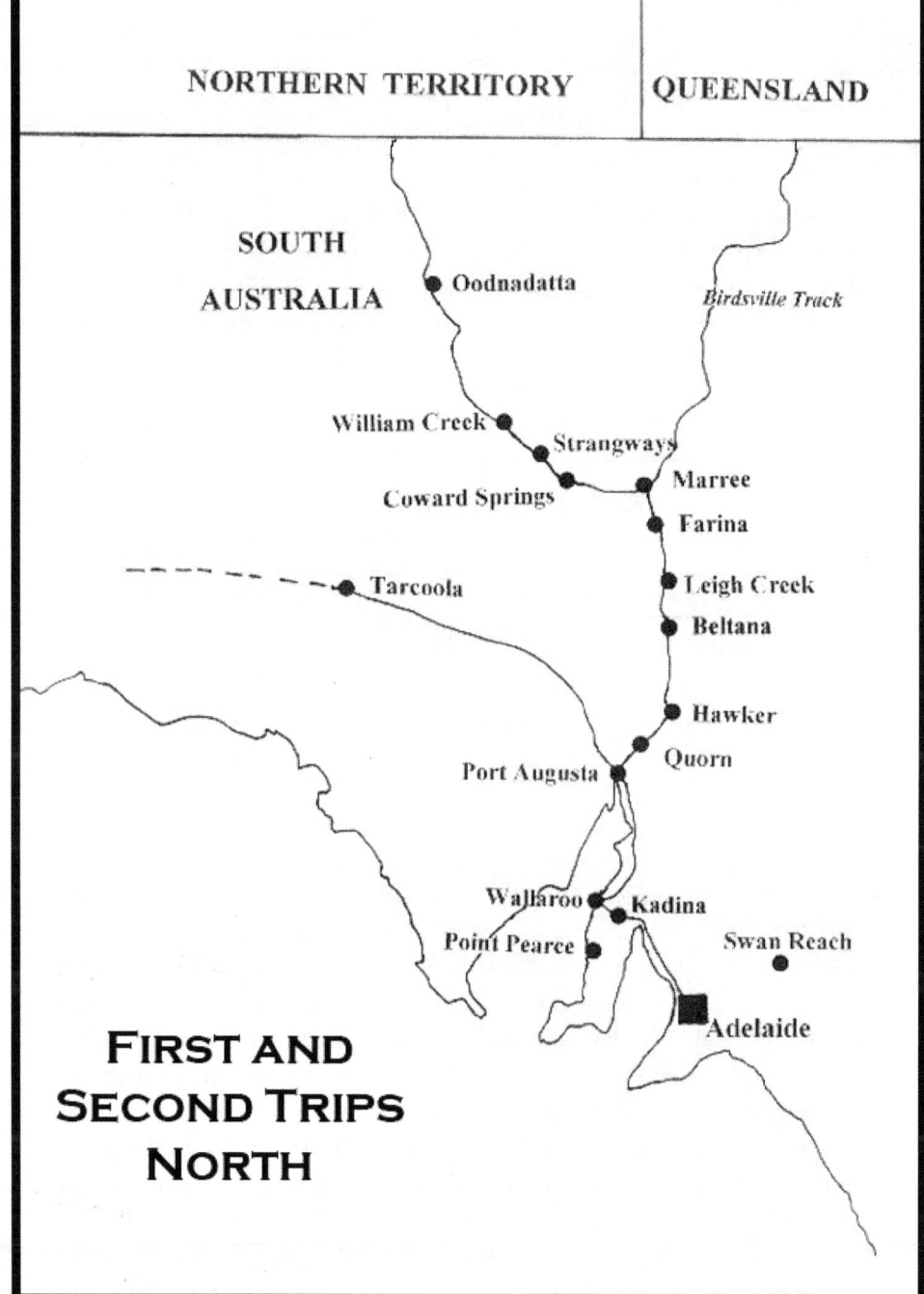

Another pamphlet was given to a young lady for her fifteen-year-old brother. She was also grateful and gave Effie 2/8d (27c) to buy more literature. In this way God provided for them to purchase the literature and blessed in the giving out of it. Eventually they headed back to Tarcoola then set out to travel approximately 200 miles (320 km) across country from the east-west railway line to the northern line heading up to Oodnadatta.

At the first station the ladies treated them very kindly and gave them a basin full of goats' milk. Effie made a custard with some of it which was the first time Colin had tasted goats' milk. It was here that Erny and Effie got the idea of having a goat to follow them so they could use the milk. However, the manager there was addicted to drink, and was not keen to tolerate missionaries too long on his station, so they soon moved on.

At the next station everything was so different with a good home and work for the Aborigines. On their arrival the men from the kitchen helped unpack their van and pitch the tent, then sent along a jug of milk and a cup full of cream. Little Colin was so excited at seeing so much cream. He said, 'Praise God for the cream, Mummy.' He was a great little singer and one day he stood up beside the manager, a man over six feet (183cm) tall and sang, 'Tell me the old, old, story of Jesus and His love.' The old gentleman was deeply touched and said, 'Well that is just marvelous for two and a half years.'

It was now late July and before they left this station there was a tremendous thunderstorm with teeming rain. They travelled on and on for miles without finding a dry place to camp. At last they reached higher ground just out of the water. Effie wrapped Colin in a blanket and sat him on the buggy seat while they attended to the donkeys and made camp. He sat there singing, 'The fight is on oh Christian soldiers', and Effie thought, 'How true, a fight for the souls of men.'

The next day they got into salt bush country and had to travel from 4.00pm right through the night until 6.00am before they were out of it, then an hour later they came to some good feed for their poor animals. They had long, wearisome belts of very stony table land country and difficult creeks to cross before they eventually reached Coward Springs, 84 miles (134km) north-west of Maree on the Northern Line.

Effie had contracted sore eyes on the cross-country trip, but was quite excited when they stopped in the township to receive a fortnight's mail.

While Erny took the donkeys several miles out to find feed Effie strained her eyes, trying to read the letters by lantern light, and began to suffer terribly with them. But Erny smeared her eyes with olive oil and prayed for them to be healed and next morning there was no sign of the problem.

There were no Aborigines at this siding so they passed on north to a big station where there were between 300 and 400 Aboriginal people. They had heard quite a lot about the wickedness and carryings on at this station and they weren't too sure what to expect. The track into it was one of the most trying they had travelled over, with the sand hills both steep and numerous.

They finally reached the station around sundown on Saturday and met the cook, a white woman who had not seen another white woman for eight years. She was understandably delighted to see Effie, but the manager was not so delighted to have a missionary on his station. Instead of receiving a welcome they were told to be off the place by Monday morning.

On the Sunday Erny gathered a huge crowd of Aborgines together, including, as in Bible times, the poor, the maimed and the blind. Using a large picture of Jesus and the children of the world he presented the gospel to them, many hearing of God's love and forgiveness for the first time and quite a few responded to his message. On Monday morning Erny and Effie felt disappointed at having to leave their Aboriginal friends so soon. Apart from this, both they and the animals were in dire need of a rest, but they committed themselves to the Lord and dutifully moved on.

Erny and Effie had earlier sketched out on the map a certain tour to do before going home and now they found much of the country better to travel over than they had anticipated. When they reached the small town at the junction with the Birdsville Track they found that, owing to anti-German sentiment over the war in Europe, the original name of Hergott Springs – named after Joseph Hergott, a German, who discovered seven artesian springs there in 1859 – had now been changed to Marree – an Aboriginal word meaning 'many possums'. Although Erny was Swiss, and therefore neutral, he made sure he didn't slip into speaking German and arouse any antipathy towards the Christian message.

After all the rough country it had bounced and jolted over their van was just about worthless by now, but the donkeys and harness were still worth something. They felt if they could just reach the township of Farina,

26 miles (42km) south of Marree, they might find a buyer for their turnout. Then they would take the train home.

Wearied from their long journeys, as they drove into the township of Farina, Erny said, 'I am really tired of giving out. I would love to just sit and listen to someone else for a change.' They hadn't heard a minister of the gospel since leaving Port Augusta eighteen months earlier. They decided to buy a loaf of baker's bread for a change and as Erny stepped into a little shop the lady kindly informed him that there was a Methodist missionary in the town and invited them along to the service.

They were delighted to meet the preacher who was well known in the north. However, he did not allow Erny to do all the listening, but asked him to take part in the service. The following Tuesday night they held another service together and shortly afterwards Erny received an offer for their turnout. It was much less than both the animals and harness had cost but they were glad to accept.

The following week Erny and Effie gratefully boarded the train for home in the midst of a terrific dust storm. In spite of this Colin was greatly impressed with their new mode of travel compared with the slowness of their donkeys. And instead of getting home just in time for Christmas, as they had promised back in autumn, the little family reached Melbourne safely in late November and were given two upstairs rooms at the back of the mission to use as their headquarters.

Chapter 6

SECOND TRIP NORTH

Soon after they arrived home, Effie's parents came down to Melbourne for the wedding of Effie's brother, Jim. Again Erny and Effie marvelled at God's hand in enabling them to be home in time for them to share in this joyous event. After the wedding Effie's parents took Colin back to the farm with them. A few weeks later Erny and Effie were able to join the family there to celebrate Christmas together, as promised.

Back at the mission, both Erny and Effie were glad to just drink in spiritual teaching and times of prayer for a while to refresh both soul and body. But before long, Erny was keen to be out and about sharing God's word wherever the opportunity arose. Around this time Effie was asked to care for an old lady who was not expected to live more than two weeks. After three months she was still with them, and Erny and Effie began to feel strongly that the Lord was calling them to return to the people of Central Australia. Effie knew what this would mean to her parents to part again so soon, and she prayed that they would understand.

Effie's father picked them up from the station and on the way home to the farm he said, 'Do you still intend to return to the wilds?' When they assured him they felt this was God's call on their lives he tried to persuade them to serve the Lord somewhere closer to home. Yet both Erny and Effie felt God's peace regarding their decision to return north.

They were warmly welcomed by everyone, although there was an underlying sadness at the thought of parting again. Then after lunch Effie's youngest sister, Emily, went to the piano and began to play and sing a song that was new to Effie,

> *'Speed away, speed away on your mission of light,*
> *To the lands that are lying in darkness and night,*
> *'Tis the Master's command, go ye forth in His name,*
> *The wonderful gospel of Jesus proclaim.*
> *Take your lives in your hand, to the work while 'tis day,*
> *Speed away! Speed away! Speed away!'*

When she had finished, Effie threw her arms around her and said, 'Em, every word of that song was for me.'

By the time their two week visit was up, the whole family was in favour of them going back. Seeing their determination to do God's will at all costs, they gave them a lovely send off and even spared Madge to return to Melbourne with them to help with their packing and wave them off on the boat to Adelaide.

On arrival in Adelaide Erny, Effie and little Colin were warmly welcomed into the home of the dear friends they had known before. They had just five shillings (50c) for their personal use and twenty-one pounds ($42) from the proceeds of their former outfit. In answer to an advertisement they were able to purchase a draper's van, and Erny quickly set to work to alter the inside of it. He painted the outside black this time to make more of a contrast, then added the same texts in white as he'd had on the first van.

They prayed for horses and were able to purchase a fine pair. When they told the dealer they would take the horses they only had five shillings (50c) in hand to pay for one week's stabling. A week later they were able to pay a deposit on the horses and little by little they were paid for and harness was made to order. Then they fitted up the van with a tent, water canteens, two camp stretchers, a portable shower and other necessary supplies.

While in Adelaide Erny and Effie attended a weekly prayer meeting and were greatly blessed and strengthened in their faith. They had more rest during their three months in Adelaide than they'd had for their six months in Victoria. While trusting God to meet all their needs, they also had a special little purse in which they kept their tithes or one tenth of all money they received. The evening before they left Adelaide they had a one pound note ($2) saved up in tithe money. Beside that they had only their train fare to the prayer meeting and wouldn't have a penny left to buy a loaf of bread to start off with in the morning.

However, they both felt they should give and the Lord would honour their faith. Effie folded the pound note up and when everyone knelt to pray, she popped it in the offering box. Before they retired that night they had twenty-five shillings ($2.50) given to them. God had again confirmed His promise to them in Luke 6:38, 'Give and it shall be given unto you, good measure, pressed down and flowing over.'

The friends with whom they were staying loaded them up with all the fruits, vegetables, jams and groceries they needed for a start off and all they needed to buy the following morning was a loaf of bread.

It was September 1916 and Colin was just over three and a half when they set out on their second trip north. At Port Wakefield they received a hearty welcome at the Methodist manse and had an opportunity to witness for the Lord in the church. Some of the friends there showed them great kindness and generosity. From there they visited the Point Pearce Aboriginal Mission Station where they spent a happy week. Some of the Aborigines there were moved in their hearts towards God and a party of them went with Erny to the beach where a number were baptised by immersion.

From there they travelled on, visiting and bearing testimony for the Master from town to town, in the different churches. At one church a friend presented them with a nearly new canvas hammock which just fitted over the top of the van to keep things dry on the road and this proved a great comfort for them in camp.

One night after leaving Port Augusta, as Colin happily ran from one to the other around the open fire, he tripped and fell, immersing his arm up to the elbow in a pot of boiling cocoa. The skin peeled off from his elbow to his finger tips. With no doctor or nurses within reach, Erny and Effie covered the arm in olive oil then prayed desperately that God would work a miracle for their little boy. And He did. The arm healed well with only a slight scar inside his elbow to show for the episode in later years.

Their horses travelled well down south on good roads, but again, the further north they went, the harder it became, as they were not used to sand and heavy country. While at Quorn Erny visited outback stations on his bike to distribute gospel literature. He was encouraged to find that people who had responded to the gospel two years previously were continuing to walk with the Lord. He had a large gathering at one camp and the Aborigines there remembered the choruses they had taught them before and sang them heartily.

On leaving Quorn, going directly north, Erny narrowly escaped a serious accident. As he was stepping up into the van, the horses suddenly started off at a gallop and Erny was thrown down beside the wheels. Effie called on the Lord and in His strength she soon pulled the horses up. Then together they thanked God that Erny was unhurt except for bruised knees.

They drove another twenty miles (32km) before pulling up for dinner at Gordon's Bridge. Erny read Matthew 6:25-34 where Jesus said not to worry about what you shall eat or drink. After lunch they had a look at the crossing and agreed, 'If the horses take us safely across it will be a miracle.' They made a start and had just got into the bed of the creek when the horses stopped and would not go any further. Evidently their work was finished.

A friendly farmer pulled the van to his house where they were kindly received. There were some donkeys about two miles (3km) away and they were taken to see them. The farmer offered to sell the horses and square up half for the donkeys and it was agreed.

During their stay there they gave the farmer a helping hand. The harness was altered and in a short time they were on the road again with three donkeys. Up to this time they had travelled from six to seven miles (about 10km) an hour with the horses but they were reduced to just two miles (about 3km) an hour. They were moving on to Leigh Creek through thunderstorms. The donkeys had a tussle, but they thanked God for providing them, for from Gordon's bridge the road grew worse and worse for miles.

When they reached Leigh Creek they were able to repurchase two of their former donkeys. After this they travelled twenty-seven miles (43km) inland from the railway line. There they pitched camp near a waterbrook and Erny assisted a bushman in erecting a bush dwelling. In return he presented them with a donkey and a milking goat.

While camped at this place they made regular visits to a local Aborigines' Camp. Soon the Indigenous people looked forward to their coming. The children learned little choruses about Jesus and His love and Erny and Effie saw a remarkable healing take place. A woman was brought from another area sick and feverish. She could hardly whisper and grew worse as the days went on. Her husband was shown the truth in James 5:14-15. He accepted God's word, and Erny anointed the woman with oil and prayed for her. The Lord healed her and she rejoiced in Jesus.. A brother of this teamster afterwards told them how he had asked Jesus to heal his baby boy when he was very feverish and 'Jesus did it' he said with joy.

One little boy, Tommy, was a wild, untameable child. By prayer and through hearing the story of Jesus, he gradually settled down and learned to love Jesus and sing from his heart of His love. Another little fellow told a white woman about Jesus. She was surprised at his knowledge and said in a letter to Effie after they had left, 'They will never forget what you have taught them.'

From here they travelled to a fairly large station where Effie was asked to cook and care for the three children while their mother was in hospital. They stayed there for nearly six months with Erny and Effie both working hard at cleaning the place up. Erny dismantled and repaired the stove which was blocked and repaired various doors and gates around the homestead. A lot of outback homesteads were neglected because the original owners had sold their property to Sir Sidney Kidman and he in turn had installed temporary managers to oversee them. As the places were not their own, they often neglected them.

Before Erny and Effie left this station the workers had a picnic in their honour and much fun was had by the stockmen as they attempted to ride Erny's donkeys through the water. Donkeys hate getting their feet wet and even the best horsebreaker had an unexpected bath.

During their time here the harness for the donkeys was repaired and Erny and Effie were presented with two more donkeys by the people with whom they were staying, making a total of eight now. On this station there were about twenty Aboriginal children whom they had told about Jesus and taught to sing many gospel choruses. As they were leaving some of the older Indigenous folk were greatly moved and asked them to return again soon.

Back on the road they met two teamsters whose children they had taught. They brought thank offerings of ten shillings each tied up in their handkerchiefs. They had many opportunities of witnessing among pastoralists and others in the bush and among outstations and many received them and their message gladly.

Travelling over tracks of hot sand at the rate of two miles (3km) an hour made it seem a long journey to cover a distance of 250 miles (400km). The food and cooking along the track were very simple and although Effie suffered much from weakness of body during this time they were grateful that no accident happened.

Along the track they met some shepherds who gladly heard the word and received literature from them. A thunderstorm was blowing up but just in time they reached an outstation where they received a hearty welcome. They stayed there for three days. However, the weather was getting worse, and after travelling sixty-five miles (104km) in five days over rough and heavy country, they were barely housed safely before the rain came down for two nights in succession, accompanied by the heaviest thunderstorm they had witnessed in their travels.

The married couple with whom they stayed believed the gospel and were refreshed in fellowship and God's word before Erny and Effie set out on the road again, rejoicing. They visited a family of bush people, contractors, camping in tents who were pleased to see them. Here they purchased a goat coming into milk as theirs was going dry. But now Erny knew he had to get Effie to Farina as soon as possible to be ready for the arrival of the new little life God was about to entrust them with.

Chapter 7

FARINA TO OODNADATTA

When they arrived at Farina many difficulties lay before them and they had to take every step by faith. Beneath a hot, scorching sun they unloaded, pitched their tent and before sundown were safely installed inside it. But the surrounding countryside was in drought, with the townspeople paying 2/6d (25c) for every hundred gallons of water hauled by road from Leigh Creek. Erny and Effie didn't have money to spend on water, yet both they and their animals were in desperate need of it.

That evening God gave them Isaiah 33:16, which ended with the words, 'His bread will be supplied and his water will not fail him.' Looking to the Lord for guidance, Erny went out to search for water and eventually came to a place in the bed of a creek where he dug down and found, to his surprise and joy, a lovely spring of water, just like rain water.

Obtaining some old drums he made a casing, put a lid on the top and had a depth of about 18" (45cm) of water which never diminished even though they used it freely. God had provided them with a soakage which met their own needs and those of their animals without them paying a penny for it. Their supply of water lasted the whole time they were camped there, yet interestingly, when the townspeople were again in need of water, they went to the site of Erny's soakage, only to find that the water was now salty and unusable.

During their stay at Farina their darling little daughter, Mary Catherine, was born on the 9th January 1918. The Lord provided the help of a trained midwife and another lady from Farina volunteered her help.

But conditions were extremely trying a fortnight before the birth with the heat registering 117F (47C) degrees in the tent, and for ten days afterwards it was 112F (44C) degrees. Yet in spite of this, mother and baby did well, and for ten months baby Mary never robbed them of a night's sleep.

By this time their van needed repairing as the front wheels had nearly collapsed. They forwarded two of the front wheels to a wheelwright with only five shillings to pay for the freight to Quorn, leaving them with one penny.

They told the Lord about it in prayer. The wheels arrived back with a bill of eight pounds fifteen shillings and three pence ($17.53). The Lord provided it and they were able to forward the amount by return mail. The firm, in sending the receipt, not knowing their circumstances, enclosed the following text of scripture, Psalm 36, 'How excellent is thy lovingkindness, oh God, therefore the children of men put their trust under the shadow of thy wings.'

When forwarding the back wheels, Erny had the freight in hand as before. The firm, hearing their testimony returned the wheels, paying the freight, and allowing 5% discount on cash. With the receipt, they sent Romans 8:35, 'Who shall separate us from the love of Christ …'

During their stay at Farina Effie was sitting on a packing case one day doing some sewing when she was bitten by a black spider. She suffered some reaction from the bite but in answer to prayer all was well again within a couple of days.

At another time their purse and bread tin were completely empty when suddenly one pound ($2) was wired to them from a minister friend. This came just in time to buy their tea before the store closed. A letter followed some days later which said, 'Trusting the offering was in time to supply your immediate need. I was prompted by God to send it by wire.'

At Farina they met only a few Aboriginals, so when Effie had recovered sufficiently they set out once more on their travels. About six miles (9km) out of Farina they had an accident, one of their goats getting under the back wheel of the van. They thought the poor animal would die, but they took it to Jesus in prayer and in the morning the goat was meekly standing beside the van. A week later she gave birth to two kids. They praised God who had given them the promise, 'Thou shalt have goat's milk enough for thy food, for the food of thy household and for the maintenance of thy maidens.' Proverbs 27:27.

One morning they discovered the donkeys had cleared off. Looking to the Lord, Erny followed their tracks over hills and gullies. He eventually found eight of them but one was still missing. Suddenly God caused it to sing out and Erny was able to find it and bring all nine safely back to the van.

They nearly got lost after leaving there, having missed the plain track for miles. They ran up against a fence and didn't know how to get back. However, finding a gate two miles (3km) further on they went through but it was a rough track. Eventually they struck the right road and at the end came across a kind bush woman who gave them a warm welcome.

Here they found an oasis in the desert, a good well of water. This woman was very industrious, and with her husband, a miner, had planted a garden and had many fowls, ducks and milking cows. With the green creepers and flowers, the homestead was very attractive and had a most refreshing effect on them after their long, dry journey. These people had not seen a missionary for about fifteen years and were extremely kind to them. It was hard to part from them.

Pressing forward over their difficult way they passed on to Salt Creek where there was water. Crossing tablelands and sandhills in all covering about 90 miles (144km) they safely reached a station where they met Aborigines they had known three years ago and they were so glad to see them again. Everyone came together and the Bible pictures and singing were thoroughly enjoyed by all.

The manager and station hands listened attentively to the gospel message and for three successive Sundays they heard the word and Erny and Effie were made welcome at the head station. When they left there they were wonderfully provided for.

The country around was at its best, green feed abounded, flowers of all description strewed the way. From here they pushed forward towards the Yellow Waterhole Sandhills – twenty-five of them, and the donkeys proved equal to the task. About sixty-five miles (104km) further on they reached another station where they were permitted to stay over Sunday and were invited to pitch their tent where they could enjoy free water, food and plenty of firewood close handy.

They were only able to visit the Aboriginal camp once a week owing to difficulties in the way. Although there were many hindrances the Indigenous people gave them a good hearing on different occasions. They met some of the West Tribe along with one old man named King George, whom they had known three years ago. He came up to the van to shake hands and told those with him that Erny and Effie were his friends which gave them an open door with the others. George also told Erny that they had given up a certain wicked practice, had not forgotten their former visit and were very pleased to see them again.

One very disastrous fear among Aborigines is the 'Black Fellows' Bone'. They imagine they have been 'boned' when they have any internal complaint or someone has a set upon them. In that frame of mind they refuse to eat and drink and just pine away through fear. But Erny explained to them that with Jesus in their heart they no longer needed to fear the effects of the 'bone'.

A boy who did not drink or smoke since he found Jesus as his Saviour told Erny that whenever he got sick, he prayed and was restored and able to work again. For four years this boy had stood firm on God's promises which was a real encouragement to Erny, seeing the seed of God's word taking root in fertile soil like this.

One woman reminded them of the woman of Samaria and told the people that she had first met Erny and Effie at another station and said, 'I believe him, you wait and see the pictures and you will believe him too.'

One man who had been brought up an infidel, said to the cook, 'I don't believe there is a God, do you?' The cook replied, 'Certainly I do, and you want to believe Him too. You go and listen to the missionary and you will learn to believe.' The unbelieving man came, listened eagerly and soon confessed that he now believed in Jesus.

Erny's aim was not to 'civilise' the Indigenous people but to show them the Light of Life, Jesus, the once crucified and now risen Saviour and soon coming King of Kings. He and Effie lifted up Jesus, praying God to prepare the hearts of the Aborigines to receive him as their Saviour and Lord. They sought continually for wisdom to make the word plain and simple for their hearers.

In September 1918 their faith was again tested. They were quite lonely, their food supplies were very low and they had only received ten shillings ($1) for the month. Effie was suffering with her feet and Colin was beginning to feel the heat. They were considering where and how they were to spend the summer, when the thought came very forcibly to Erny,

'Send your wife and little ones home for the summer.' He didn't like to think of Effie travelling alone, yet could not see that he could leave all their belongings to go with them. However, early in October he mentioned his conviction to Effie and they took it to the Lord in prayer.

They realised, too, that something must be done about Colin. He was now over five and a half years old and they knew they should be making plans for his schooling. They didn't have a penny toward travelling nor had their food supply been replenished. However the next morning in prayer Effie received such a sure witness in her spirit that this was the right decision that she began asking the Lord to show them the date when she was to go.

They took Colin in their arms and explained to him that when little boys were six years old they had to go to school and that they were going to take him home to Grandpa and Grandma, but that they did not have a penny towards it and if God did not send the money they could not go. So Colin began to pray, 'Dear Lord, will you please send us all the money we need to take us home to Ma and Pa?'

The next mail brought them four pounds ten shillings ($9) and in less than a fortnight they had over eight pounds ($16). A few days later a young Christian, not knowing a thing about their circumstances, drove up to their tent with 25 lbs (40kg) of flour, sugar, tea, jam, tins of salmon and tinned fruit. At the next station after an encouraging gospel service, Effie had an envelope placed in her hand containing three pounds ten shillings ($7).

They journeyed on and when they arrived at Oodnadatta, where they were to catch the train, they received numbers of letters from friends and practically every one contained an offering. Then a wire came from a dear brother with ten pounds ($20). When all this was reckoned up they had enough for all their fares to Adelaide, Erny included.

Then the poorest woman in the town came and asked them in for a meal and readily opened her shed for their van and boxes. A young man from the nearest station took charge of their donkeys and they realised that the way had marvellously opened up for a furlough. Their Heavenly Father had 'done far more abundantly above all that they could ask or think.'

Chapter 8

THIRD TRIP NORTH

On reaching Melbourne Erny and Effie were relieved to hear that the armistice ending four years of bloodshed, known as the Great War, had been signed on the 11th November 1918. But now an influenza epidemic, which had begun in America the previous March, was sweeping the world. It was feared more lives would be lost from influenza than the twenty million estimated to have died in the war.

With the flu now raging in Melbourne, Erny and Effie were prevented from testifying in many of the places they had planned to visit. After a refreshing break among loved ones both in Melbourne and Gippsland, Ernie and Effie felt the Lord laying on their hearts once again the burden to return to the work he had called them to up north. Bidding farewell to family for the third time, they especially felt the tug of leaving six year old Colin with his grandparents.

On the 19th May 1919 they set out with sixteen-month-old Mary for Oodnadatta. Arriving in Adelaide they were again welcomed by the loving, saintly old couple who, during each visit, had provided for them as if they were their own children.

Breaking their northerly train journey at Quorn, Erny set out to distribute gospel literature on his bike. He then cycled out to the various Aboriginal camps they had visited two years previously. These people were full of joy and quite excited at seeing Erny again and he was able to hold some wonderful gatherings with them. He was quite heartened to find that the dear little Aboriginal children remembered the choruses they had taught them earlier and sang along most heartily.

The drought had continued in the north and on their return to Oodnadatta much of Erny's time was spent mustering and shepherding their two goats and eight donkeys, trying to find feed for them. Yet the Aborigines were always ready to gather together for a meeting to sing choruses and hear God's word.

Then suddenly the Indigenous people began to fall sick with influenza. They were so neglected and dying helplessly like animals that Erny's heart went out to them. With help from the local doctor and policeman, Erny and Effie rigged up an isolation camp outside the town. Then, with four donkeys pulling the van, Erny went out and gathered up the sick Aborigines, bringing them into the camp where they could be cared for.

Many were carried in one day in hope and carried out later as a corpse. A hole was dug outside the town and the body was rolled in its blankets and buried, many without the knowledge of a Saviour, without hope in God. Some were so terrified that, after their first night in camp they ran away, choosing to die alone in the bush.

Erny and Effie had a busy time for about six weeks nursing and caring for those still alive until the epidemic gradually eased. Yet they lost no opportunity to tell the sufferers of the great love of Jesus who died to save them all. As it drew to a close they gave heartfelt thanks to God that He had upheld and protected them and in spite of daily contact with the disease neither they nor little Mary had come down with it.

During this time of spiritual and physical strain, their financial position was also very trying, but they continued to look to the Lord to meet their needs. Eighteen months ago they had prayed about an extra little cart which they needed to carry water and wood while in camp and to take some of their luggage when travelling to leave more room in the van for Effie and Mary. At this time Christian friends in Adelaide provided for the purchase of a little donkey and harness. Money then came in enabling Erny to buy two wheels and shafts, the axle was given to him and he made a cart out of a strong draper's case. When all was put together it provided them with just the little cart they had been needing.

Their van and harness then had to be overhauled, repaired, and set up for the out-back country, for now they were about to leave the head of the railway line at Oodnadatta and go north in a real step of faith. They set out on the 1st August, 1919, and were amazed at the kindness and generosity shown to them by the townspeople. They had not been able to buy fruit for the journey, but one young lady came to their van with half a case of juicy navel oranges and apples. And so the Lord provided for them all along the way.

They had many opportunities to hold gospel services at various stations along the way, with the white people gathering for a service as well as the Aborigines. At one station the mother gathered her children for a service, and following it Erny had the great joy of dedicating her little girl to the Lord.

Summer had now begun and each week the sun grew hotter and their way became very wearying. The country varied; at times they had good roads, clear tracks and found water and wood easily at short stages. Then came trying times, struggling through dry creek beds, steep sandhills, rough, stony and bare tablelands with little feed and long stages without water. Yet they had God's promise, that, 'He will not suffer us to be tempted above that we are able to bear'.

Sometimes the water would be off the track and difficult for new travellers to find. One day they missed a watering place and became very discouraged, thinking of the distance they had yet to go to the next water. The thirsty animals were hard to drive, the sand was heavy, the sun fierce and the goats knocked up, with their tongues hanging out, yet they had no water to give them. Erny was quite disheartened, then suddenly Effie sensed God's presence and began to sing,

> *'Too oft a weary and discouraged,*
> *We pour a sad complaint,*
> *Believing in a living Saviour,*
> *Why should we ever faint?'*

Erny immediately felt uplifted. They had this experience repeatedly, that they were never down together. Before they were married the Lord had given Effie the promise in Ecclesiastes 4:9-10, 'Two are better than one ... for if they fall, the one will lift up his fellow', and many times they had proved this to be so.

Outback Evangelist

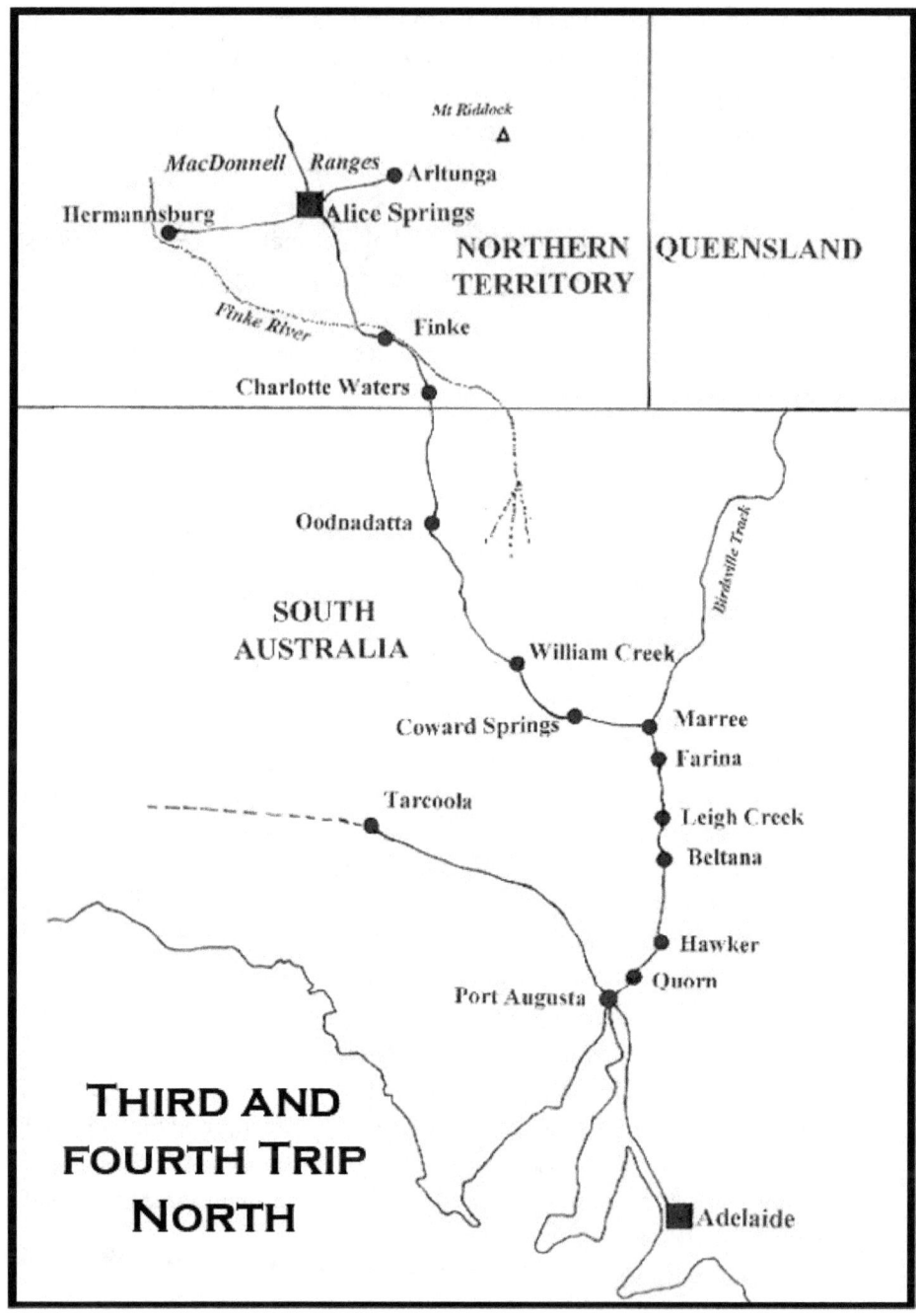

Another day while travelling along they tried many times to find water in a dry gum creek but were unsuccessful. There was no indication of water at all, but Effie said, 'Let us go on until eleven o'clock,' for it was Saturday and if it could be avoided they never travelled on a Sunday but observed it to the Lord. Just then they came to another crossing and on both sides they saw pretty wild flowers and the best feed they had seen all along the road, but still no water. Erny said, 'I'll have one more try while you boil the billy.' Off he went with his shovel and before the billy boiled he found water in two places.

He came back full of joy, had lunch, unharnessed the animals and returned to dig deeper. In a little while he had a lovely soakage with beautiful clear water – plenty for them and their thirsty animals, and they glorified the Lord who had given them water in the wilderness.

Rising early on Sunday morning they went to their little soakage and underneath the beautiful gums had a special time of praise and thanksgiving for this quiet resting place, which the Lord in His loving mercy had provided for them.

As they travelled on they came to nine or ten ponds in succession of beautiful clear water. They were called "Ducks' Ponds" where the pelicans and waterhens were at home, and round about mobs of cattle were feeding and resting, satisfied. The sight was inspiring after travelling through dry desert lands for miles and miles. They had one of the prettiest drives for about four miles (6km) passing from pond to pond, with reeds and rushes and flourishing gums and abundance of water not often experienced in the Far North.

Another time they had a terrible struggle to get over thirty-five miles (56km) of heavy, sandy country, with many dry creeks to cross. The donkeys were two days without water, the days were so hot they could only travel very early in the morning and then after sundown for a few hours. One morning the donkeys refused to go on after 10.00am, and just as they set them free a fierce north wind arose and continued for the whole day as though it were off a fire. They could not quench their thirst, an unpleasant taste was in their mouths, and everywhere they looked there was red sand. The sun went down but the temperature in the van remained at 107F (42C) degrees.

They harnessed up the donkeys and pressed on though. At 11.00pm they had to cross a dry river. They were right into the bed of it when suddenly the animals were too overcome to go further. They had to let them go and camp. They were still five to seven miles (8-10km) from water and there was nothing to prevent the donkeys from leaving them in their search for water. Erny and Effie cried out to God.to hold them, knowing that He had power over all flesh. They boiled their billy for supper and still had a pannikin of water left to refresh their three faces before settling at 1.30am in the bed of that white, sandy river. They felt so distressed that Effie said with tears, 'I would not care if the flood came down tonight and we were no more heard of.'

After three hours' rest they arose to find the donkeys nearby and soon had them harnessed. God gave them strength and by 8.30am they reached a well of water where they stayed for four days and met white men and quite a number of Aborigines who told them that this place had frequent dust storms. But God held them off and as they were leaving they were told that they never remembered being so free from dust storms before.

The next stage was fifty-five miles (88km) to Alice Springs with no known water along the way. Daily they prayed for rain, but in spite of thunder and lightning, only a few drops fell. They set off each evening at 7.00pm and when it grew too dark to see the track, Effie walked ahead with a lantern until the moon rose. For two whole nights they travelled like this and rested through the heat of the day, although the flies and heat were too great to allow them much sleep. Yet little Mary was able to sleep and was well and happy right through this time.

The third day at 2.00pm on the 16th December they reached water in the centre of Australia. Towards the end their little goats took a lot of coaxing, lying down in the shade of every tree. They had kept up really well through the long, wearisome journey, and gave milk all the time, which was a great provision for both Effie and Mary.

All around this well were mobs of camels. The owners said they were poor travellers in the night and would stamp their feet and throw their load in the heat of the day. When Erny and Effie heard this they were filled with gratitude for their brave little animals who had brought them safely through.

They praised God for opportunities to share stories of His love with the Aborigines along the way, some hearing it for the first time ever. Others they had met four years ago in Pt Augusta greeted them with beaming faces and told them they remembered the teachings about the love of Jesus. They were always very attentive and never grew tired of seeing the Bible pictures and hearing the stories. In spite of all the difficulties, Erny's and Effie's hearts rejoiced in God's goodness and the opportunities He had given them to share His message with many who had never before heard it.

Chapter 9

ALICE SPRINGS

As Erny and Effie neared Alice Springs they felt that God would have them rest there for the remainder of the summer. Alice Springs was a pretty little bush township at the foot of the MacDonnell Ranges which stretch for some 300 miles (480km) east and west of it. Situated virtually in the red centre of Australia the town was named for Lady Alice Todd, wife of Sir Charles Heavitree Todd, builder of the Overland Telegraph line, after whom the Todd River and Heavitree Gap were named.

The town consisted of a hotel, store, police station, half-castes' bungalow and a scattering of white-washed houses. It boasted a population of twenty-one white people – Effie making the seventh white woman – around fifty half-castes, and 300 to 400 Aboriginals scattered around the area.

They were made welcome by the postmaster near the Overland Telegraph Station and pitched their tent in one of the prettiest spots, right under huge palms with pepper and gum trees all around. They called this place 'Palm Rest' and they enjoyed a calm, refreshing rest and change from travelling.

They had only been there for five days when the drought broke. The thunder rolled and crashed, the lightning flashed and the rain poured down. Now they could see why God didn't send the rain two weeks earlier for the Todd River was soon in flood and it would have been impossible for them to cross it. God in His wisdom had withheld the rain and enabled them to cover fifty-five miles (88km) of red, sandy desert without finding any water.

Erny was invited to visit the school for half-castes and spent many happy hours there teaching the children. How they loved to sing. He also had many opportunities to meet Aboriginals who were always coming and going from fifty to ninety miles (80-144km) around.

Erny and Effie chose to hold their services under a huge gum tree. When the Aboriginals saw them driving along to this tree with one donkey in their little cart they would come running from all directions, old and young, men and women with babies on their backs. They would often have over fifty in their gathering. The Aboriginals would spread a bag or blanket out for Erny and Effie to sit on then they would all sit down on the ground in circles to hear about Jesus who shed His blood upon the cross for all people of all nations.

After the rain, feed soon grew in abundance and their animals got quite fat. They all had real rest for their natural bodies and such a refreshing from the presence of the Lord.

In May 1920 Erny and Effie broke up their bush home to go out 70 miles (112km) east to the Arltunga Goldfields, not for the gold that perishes but for precious souls. Oh what a change in travelling. They now had beautiful feed and water all the way. As they visited stations along the track they had many opportunities to sow seeds for the Master in the hearts of both Indigenous and white folk. They emphasised that God was no respecter of persons and that the blood of Jesus Christ alone can wash sin from the heart.

There was one burly bushman who had not been to the city for at least twenty-five years. His outward appearance was rough and careless and he seemed to fear nothing. Erny was warned, 'He is Irish, don't talk to him, it's no use.' But when Erny was able to have a heart-to-heart talk with the man and offered him a New Testament the man exclaimed, 'I have been wanting one of these for years so now I will study it and see for myself.'

To reach the farthest station 125 miles (200km) to the north-east where there was a white family they had to pass over some very rough stretches of the MacDonnell Ranges. At one place the rocks and ruts were so dangerous that they had to look moment by moment to the Lord to keep them safe. At night they would hear the wild dogs mournfully howling all around them. One morning, while Erny was mustering the donkeys, their goats took fright and ran away into the ranges. There was no sign or sound of them, but the noise of the wild dogs was terrible. However, God protected the goats and Erny was eventually able to find them and bring them safely back to the van.

The way was extremely difficult and they began to wonder what reception they would receive at journey's end, for the reports that had been told them of this family were not encouraging. But God gave them the joy to sing from their hearts,

> *'There's surely somewhere a lonely place*
> *In earth's harvest field so wide,*
> *Where I may labour through life's short day*
> *For Jesus, the crucified.*
> *So trusting my all to Thy tender care,*
> *And knowing Thou lovest me,*
> *I'll do Thy will with a heart sincere,*
> *I'll be what You want me to be.'*

At last they reached the station and the welcome given would never be forgotten. A homely woman, so neat and clean, with a heart full of love and open arms came out to meet them and welcomed them in to their small bush home. Her children were very shy at first but were soon playing happily with little Mary.

Erny and Effie stayed with them for several days and had some blessed times in sharing the words of life to these dear white people in the way-backs. They were happy and contented and the loving mother was teaching her children Bible stories and Sankey's hymns. They thanked God for their visit and on leaving they loaded Erny and Effie up with good food for the rough journey back. To meet such loving friends away in the never-nevers did their hearts good and helped them to forget the toils of the road.

One morning while they were staying there, Erny visited Mt Riddock (or Rambarrambarra, its Aboriginal name), one of the highest peaks in the Eastern MacDonnell Ranges. He climbed right to the top amid grasses and pines and there he worshiped God. It was just heavenly and Erny felt moved to ask of God the heathen round about for His inheritance.

There lay all around him a far-stretching plain with huge scrub ninety miles (144km) across and three hundred miles (480km) long. In rainy seasons it was a fertile country, but was mostly dry without wells or creeks. To the south-east and west lay the MacDonnell Ranges, in all their grandeur. But the cry of his heart went out to God for the many tribes of Aborigines, unknown to him but not to the One who gave His life for them. Oh how Erny longed to reach those people scattered some hundred miles (160km) further east who had never been told of the love of Jesus.

Erny and Effie returned to Alice Springs along the same tracks, meeting with Aborigines here and there as they journeyed along. At one place an older Aboriginal woman who had heard them speak before walked nine miles (15km) with a three-year-old child on her back just to hear them a second time.

On their first Sunday back in Alice Springs they again had fifty local Aborigines at their meeting and all felt the presence of the Lord in a wonderful way.

Chapter 10

HERMANNSBURG

The following week they left for the Hermannsburg Mission Station on the Finke River, ninety miles (144km) to the south-west. The track was indistinct and people could not remember when a vehicle had last passed that way. But they looked to the Lord to guide them. From one particular well their directions were, 'Strike out west and look for a track'. This they did but went quite a distance without seeing a wheel mark. At last they cried out to God, knowing what it would mean if they failed to find the track to water. Suddenly God's Spirit came upon Effie and she began to sing,

'Wonderful, wonderful Jesus,
Oh, He's a wonderful Saviour,
Bless His holy name.'

Right there and then old tracks appeared before them and they knew they were on the right road.

Another time they came to a parting of the ways and counted twelve buggy tracks leading off in different directions. They stopped, closed their eyes and asked God which track to take. As they opened their eyes there was a beautiful rainbow over one track and they felt that was God's sign to take that one. They did the ninety miles (144km) in five and a half days and safely reached the Hermannsburg Mission Station, saying with grateful hearts, 'Jesus led us all the way'.

They were heartily welcomed by Pastor Carl Strehlow and his wife, Frieda, their thirteen-year-old son, Ted, and their co-labourers. Erny and

Effie spent eleven happy days with chosen people of God who had left all to follow Him. They in return thanked God for sending Erny and Effie all that way – 400 miles (640km) from the terminus of the Northern Railway – into their midst.

The Hermannsburg mission consisted of 1200 square miles of land which earlier missionaries had planted with date palms and other fruit trees to provide food for the missionaries and their helpers. Here, for the first time, Erny and Effie heard a service in the Aranda (now Arrente) Aboriginal tongue. Pastor Carl Strehlow, who had arrived at Hermannsburg in Oct 1894, had developed a written form of the Aranda language and had recently completed his six-year translation of the New Testament into the Aranda language. He had also published a seven volume work, begun in 1907, about the Aranda and Loritja tribes.

In the evenings the Indigenous children would sit in a circle around their teacher and sing hymn after hymn firstly in English then in Aranda. It was beautiful and made the tears flow. Erny and Effie were blessed spiritually, as well as bodily with good food and a comfortable bed. It was hard to part with those dear ones. When Erny and Effie left, everyone sang, 'We'll never say Good-bye'. Then quite a number of the Aborigines followed them for over two miles (3km), singing parting hymns.

The Hermannsburg Mission Station

Erny and Effie finally reached Alice Springs for the third time, but only stayed briefly this time while they made preparations for their next journey south-west. In the evening, as they went to rest, it was so encouraging to hear the Aboriginal folk and especially the children, away in the distance singing the gospel choruses they had learned. In the day-time the children would come running to their camp to see three year old Mary who was always delighted to see them and would imitate her daddy, giving each a little book and saying, 'Now, children, all look to Mary,' and they would in all sincerity look to her as a little teacher and sing away so sweetly together.

When Erny and Effie were saying good-bye to a dear soul in Alice Springs who loved the Lord, she thanked them very much for their visit and help to her and said, 'Never give up your noble work Mr Kramer.' Then she clasped Effie in her arms, saying, 'Good-bye darling. If we don't meet here again we will meet with the Lord,' and they parted with tears of joy.

Going south-west they had some of the roughest country to pass through and for seventy miles (112km) it was necessary to have an Aboriginal boy for a pilot. There was a real change in the season too. Instead of scorching sun they now had cool weather and thunderstorms. But the Lord withheld the heavy rains until they were safely housed under an iron roof. They stayed there for a fortnight, receiving great kindness from rough bushmen.

From there their journey was quite a pleasure. Water was plentiful at easy stages, melons, which were good food for animals, were in abundance, and wild flowers were everywhere. The desert for miles and miles was blossoming as a rose. Erny and Effie had seen the country at its worst and now it was at its best, the birds sang sweetly while the animals skipped about full of life.

On their journey south they came across a man with his lip badly cut. He had been kicked by a horse. Erny was enabled, by the grace of God, to put two stitches in it and praised God when the lip healed perfectly.

Their van had become a black and white ambulance, firstly to carry the Aborigines in the flu epidemic and now to transport an unfortunate white man who had been very badly burnt, more than 100 miles (160km) to Oodnadatta for treatment. It was a fearful case, but they prayed for the man and God gave him a marvellous recovery.

Erny and Effie's last summer during this time in the north was spent relieving friends at an eating house and store during a time of family distress. While there they prayed much about the further development of their efforts for the Aborigines, and waited on God to know His mind in the matter.

In December 1921 Erny and Effie received news from home that a great revival was spreading in Melbourne. The mission where they had laboured was in need of workers and Erny and Effie were asked if they would be willing to come back and help. They were both in need of spiritual and physical refreshment, so after much prayer, they wrote back agreeing to help with the work there for however long the Lord should appoint.

Chapter 11

A NEW VISION

On their arrival in Melbourne Erny and Effie became good friends with Mr Bob Davis and his wife of Heidelberg. They had a daughter about the same age as Colin and they invited the family to come and live with them.

Erny and Effie soon found themselves in the midst of much activity at the mission headquarters in Melbourne with plenty to occupy them both spiritually and in practical ways. Effie's youngest brother, Alex, had recently married Leila, daughter of the mission leader, and it was decided to build a three storey house alongside the mission as a home for Alex and Leila, and with accommodation for visiting evangelists and others in need.

Mr John Cavell, a top brick layer, did the job, with Erny as his off-sider, mixing mortar and laying bricks. This experience with a top tradesman gave Erny the knowledge he needed later on to build their home and church in Alice Springs. His final lesson along this line came on their return trip through Adelaide where Erny saw people at Christies Beach making bricks with beach sand and lime, using wooden moulds then sun-baking the bricks.

The building in Melbourne was completed in time to accommodate a visiting evangelist from Britain, followed shortly afterwards by one from America. Erny played a leading role in the organisation of these meetings, and both he and Effie were deeply encouraged and renewed in their own faith as they saw many lives touched for the Lord in a wonderful way during this time.

Yet in spite of the blessings in Melbourne, they both realised that the fire still burned strongly in their hearts for the north country and its people. Erny felt the Lord laying on his heart a vision for a permanent centre to be established in Alice Springs where a home for missionaries could be opened and from which evangelistic trips could be made to outlying areas. He hoped, in time, to establish a scriptural knowledge institution along the pattern of the late George Muller's Institution, with a shelter for full-blooded Aboriginal orphans, who at that time were sadly neglected.

Friends urged Erny to bring these matters before the church and trust God to supply what was needed to bring his vision about. A Christian coachbuilder offered to build a suitable van most reasonably for the heavy and dangerous track north, with storage spaces for their equipment and special sides that could be rolled up to allow any breeze to flow through. Friends presented them with a portable organ for Effie to play and a kind lady provided them with a 'magic lantern' so they could show slides of Bible stories to the people of the north.

In December 1922 Erny and Effie had hands laid on them and prayer was offered on their behalf for the service they had been called to. Then, putting their new buggy on the train with them, they travelled back to Adelaide, this time with Colin joining them. With the thought of being permanently settled in Alice Springs now, ten-year-old Colin and five-year-old Mary would be able to attend the school there run by Mrs Ida Standley for both white and half-caste children.

In Adelaide they spent four months making final preparations for their journey north. During this time Erny spoke in numerous churches, and to many Christian Endeavour and Sunday School groups on 'Mission Work in the Heart of Australia.'

The whole family had been cared for in a most comfortable home and as the time for their departure drew near Effie became rather anxious and fearful. Another special addition to their family was expected in a few months and what lay ahead of her just seemed too much to face. Then one day, while in prayer, Effie felt the Lord challenging her with the thought that He had kept them and provided for them in the past, and therefore was able to do the same for them in the future. As Effie acknowledged this, she said, 'Lord, I'm willing to go.'

Going to Erny she said, 'My dear, you are the stronger in the Lord and in body, so whatever the Lord makes plain to you, do, and I will be willing.' As Erny prayed, several passages of scripture came strongly to his mind, 'Arise and go!', 'Obey we must' and 'Thy will be done.' Then the joy and peace of God rolled over their souls.

The very next day as Erny stepped into Bible House on business, he was surprised to meet up with both the President and Secretary of the Aborigines Friends Association who immediately offered to send the family and their van on the boat to Port Augusta. Two weeks later Erny and Effie had their farewell meeting with those in their little mission hall where they were showered with love and the promise of the people's prayers. They were also informed that five large boxes of groceries were being sent on the boat with them so they would have plenty to eat when they reached Port Augusta.

On the morning of their departure Erny and Effie were awakened by a voice at the window saying, 'Brother Kramer, I am leaving a camp sheet on the window sill for you, fare ye well,' and the kind donor wheeled away on his bicycle.

When they reached the wharf at Port Adelaide a large crowd had gathered from the various churches where Erny had preached. Erny, Effie and the children were laden down with gifts of fruits, lollies, jam and biscuits, plus a portable shower bath which was presented to them by a dear Christian lady. They watched as their brand new caravan was lifted by five strong ropes and settled safely on the deck of the steamer. Then their well wishers joined them in a gospel song, all with tears streaming down their faces, before the four of them climbed aboard the Steamship *Paringa*. God had indeed done more abundantly than they had even asked or thought.

All went well on the voyage and they reached Port Augusta about 7.30am on the 27th March 1923. Leaving his family and luggage on board, Erny set out to buy some horses to pull their wagon but with no success. He then walked to the suburb where they had pitched their tents nine years earlier, but now there were houses everywhere. He knelt on a nearby sandhill and committed the problem to the Lord. Shortly afterwards he met a Christian gentleman who offered his vacant allotment about one and a half miles (2km) out of town on which to pitch their tents. Erny thanked him, then hired a motor lorry to carry them and their luggage and tow the caravan to the allotment.

It was a special spot with huge pepper trees for shade, As an added bonus they discovered their neighbour was a Salvation Army sister who was kindness itself to them. In a short time they had a comfortable little home made of tents, one for the kitchen and one for the bedroom, a shelter for the caravan, and a playground for the children with a swing and hammock, all under the welcome shade of the feathery pepper trees.

Erny had decided to try and travel as far north as they could with horses, keeping mainly to the track beside the railway line, as travelling with the donkeys was so slow. Soon after their arrival Erny met up with the man from whom they had bought their first four donkeys nine years ago and to Erny's astonishment he had five horses for sale at a cost of 44 pounds ($88). They only had five pounds ($10) in hand, given them three months previously with the words, 'for your horses', otherwise their cash box was empty. After a time of prayer, Erny felt moved to accept them in faith, with the promise ringing in his mind, 'My God shall supply all your need.'

He explained the situation to the man and after a moment's hesitation he shook Erny's hand and said he was willing to trust him and allowed him to leave the horses in his fields until he was ready to take them. Twelve days later Erny was able to pay another ten pounds ($20), then four ($8) more, but after that nothing more came in. Then one day a letter came from a Christian man in Adelaide who said, 'Re your horses : the Lord is paying for them. Just say if you are in need of the money at once. If not I will bring it to you, God willing, next week.'

When he arrived the following week their friend handed them the exact amount outstanding, twenty-five pounds ($50). He told them he didn't know where it had come from, but that when he had written to them he had received the assurance from the Lord that the horses would be paid for. They had a precious night of fellowship together and as Erny farewelled their friend the following morning, his eyes filled with tears. God had indeed been faithful in answering their prayers and meeting this need.

On the 12th June they were blessed by the arrival of a little daughter whom they named Euphemia Faith. Effie had a difficult time during the birth and feared she was not going to survive, but the Lord spoke to her heart the words, 'My flesh and my heart fails, but God is the strength of my heart and my portion forever.' Then the Lord's presence enveloped her and with the kind help of her nurse Effie was safely delivered of her little one.

When Faith was one month old a friend very kindly loaned Erny a buggy and pony to take the family to a missionary meeting in the Presbyterian Church, and from then on they never missed an opportunity to meet with various church people. Soon after this the Methodists, Presbyterians and Salvation Army united for prayer and preparation for a ten days' mission in their town with Erny as the speaker.

Erny and Effie also had many happy times with the Aboriginal people, meeting them in ones and twos in the hospital and other places, and having camp meetings with them. The numbers varied as there were only about a dozen living at the actual port. One lad told Erny that he had given his heart to Jesus nine years ago when Erny knelt with him in his tent. He had never forgotten that experience and wanted to learn more.

They also heard about a Aboriginal woman who had been a slave to drink when they were in Port Augusta nine years ago. She was a splendid sewing and laundry woman and she made many a try to live a good life, but failed again and again. They had spent some difficult days and nights with her but eventually they had left the port fearing she was a hopeless case. Later they heard that she had attended meetings at the Salvation Army and had finally given her life to the Lord. From then on she had lived a bright, happy, useful life in the service of the Lord for some four years before she died a peaceful death in the Port Augusta Hospital. Many had admired her faith.

The family received much kindness from the townspeople during their stay and made many new friends. One lady gave Effie a delightful birthday party, providing the opportunity for her to share with those present about their work amongst the Aborigines. This family arranged for Effie and the three children to stay with them for their final week in Port Augusta. That meant Erny could more readily dismantle their little camp and pack their things. These included a new little stove and copper plus various kitchen utensils they had bought in Port Augusta for their proposed new home. All were packed into boxes ready to go by railway and pack camels to Alice Springs. Until now Effie had done the washing in a kerosene tin and cooked in a camp oven, so these things were a real luxury to her.

When the time came for their departure, their friends' house was filled with well wishers bringing parcels of food for the road. Faith was nine weeks old, and as the little family set off on their northward journey, Erny's and Effie's hearts were filled to overflowing at the goodness of God.

Chapter 12

TRIALS AND BLESSINGS

A lady in Port Augusta had told Erny and Effie that she had lived on the first station they would come to for twenty-five years. It was only twenty-five miles (40km) from the port, and in all that time neither a missionary nor minister had ever called on them. On their arrival they were made welcome for the week-end in the men's hut, and although the men were very busy shearing they had the opportunity to hold two services with the working men and with the shearers at the shed. They all accepted little gospels provided by the British and Foreign Bible Society. However, Erny and Effie were told that the hut was a home for various snakes and on the Sunday night a four foot long brown snake was killed there. By the time they left they were praising the Lord for keeping them all safe.

At the next station they received a royal welcome from the couple in charge of the domestic duties there. In the evening all the working people gathered in the kitchen where they enjoyed a hearty sing of the good old hymns and listened intently to the gospel being preached. When it came time to leave, the people loaded them up with fresh food and special offerings to use when the need arose.

From there on to Hawker they had little opportunity to share the gospel as the people they met were busy shearing. Two miles out of Hawker they were made welcome at a farm where they were able to hold a service and stay for the weekend. Again they were loaded up with good fresh food from the farm as they left.

At Beltana they were warmly welcomed by the Rev W Gray and the matron of the AIM hostel, and all along the way they were received with much kindness, both white and Indigenous people glad to hear again the preaching of God's word and to receive Christian reading material.

At Anna Creek Station they retired for the night at 10.00pm with a calm, clear sky. Then about 1.00am a dust storm suddenly arose and blew up a hurricane which continued until daylight. The pigs were squealing, the dogs howling, the windmill creaking, sheets of iron flapping, and they were almost suffocated with the red dust and sand. They enjoyed the home comforts of the station the next day and appreciated their help in cleaning and preparing everything once more for their onward journey.

Further dust storms made their journey extremely difficult. With the hot weather setting in they began rising between 3.00 and 4.00am so they could travel in the early hours of the morning. They did the same in the cool hours of the evening. But the strain began to tell on the horses and finally Jinnie, their saddle horse, after groaning with pain, just lay down flat on the ground and made no effort to rise again. They could not spare the horse, so they laid hands on her and prayed for the Lord to restore her. Within two hours she got up and began to look for feed. In the morning she was ready to go on again. They went steadily on to the next waterhole where they rested up for the weekend.

The other horses were exhausted, and they had to give them time to rest along the way. They had planned to reach Oodnadatta in daylight but it was really dark when they arrived and, losing his way, Erny found they were right up against the railway fence. Turning, he saw a light and found the lady who had invited them to stay with her when they arrived, standing by her gate with a lantern. She had been watching for them since before sundown and it was now 9.00pm. They spent one week there which proved to be a time of refreshing for both the family and their horses.

They spent a happy time in Oodnadatta, meeting old and new friends, several pressing gifts and offerings into their hands to help with the work. They had the pleasure of holding a magic lantern meeting at the Presbyterian Hostel. Many Aboriginal faces could be seen at the rear and the next day they implored the police officer to ask Erny to show the pictures again. So the following night they held a second meeting, this time at the police station. Owing to the numbers and the closeness indoors, the meeting was held outside, with the visitors seated on the lawns. By request, they also held a service in the hostel schoolroom on the Sunday night. On each occasion the attendance was very good, and people's hearts were stirred by the Bible pictures and the message Erny gave afterwards.

Again, as they set out, they were replenished with much good, fresh food, having received apples and welcome navel oranges from Adelaide. Their hostess also gave them five fowls for their start in Alice Springs.

The horses were in fairly good condition after a week's rest and they started out quite well, but they were beyond the rail head now, and on their second day out they met up with a large mob of cattle watering at the bore. When they set out to continue on their way, the track had been completely obliterated by the cattle. After a while they found what they thought was the track, only to discover later that they were on a dry road and travelled fifty miles (80km) in the extreme heat without water or feed for the animals.

Next morning Erny left the family in the van with the small amount of water that remained and set out on his saddle horse, Jinnie, driving the other horses, to try and find food and water for them. After several hours of ploughing through deep sand for about 15 miles (24km) he finally noticed some bush horses apparently heading for water. Following them, he soon found a pool of green, muddy water, but it helped to revive the horses. By the time Erny eventually found his way back to the van he had been gone for more than six hours and the heat and strain had told on him so much that he was too faint to eat or drink for some time. After a while the children were able to coax him to take small mouthfuls of a juicy orange and gradually he revived enough to travel a few miles more until sundown.

The next day was very trying but they finally reached Hamilton Bore and here they found beautiful water beneath shady gums for all to enjoy. However, there was not a blade of grass there for the animals and when they reached the next watering place they found it had dried up. The following morning at daybreak Erny once more left the van and set out with the almost expiring horses, coaxing them slowly along for seven hours over the 14 miles (24km) to the Federal Station where there was good feed and water.

The following morning Erny led the weakened horses over the 12 miles (20km) to the Bloods Creek homestead. Here Mr Bill Bayles loaned Erny three big fresh horses so he could return and bring the caravan to the station. But the three days Erny had been gone had been an extremely anxious time for Effie, trying to care for the three children and the smaller animals while not knowing what had happened to Erny and the horses.

At Bloods Creek Station they received a very kind welcome from old friends. Owing to the drought and the severe state of the road ahead, they gratefully accepted the kind invitation of Mr and Mrs Bill Bayles to rest there awhile.

But the heat and strain of the journey had finally proved too much for Effie and while there she suffered a complete breakdown. They considered taking her to the Oodnadatta hospital, but she became too ill to manage the journey.

They were told that the wife at the next station had much experience in bush nursing, so, making a bed for Effie in the van, Erny carefully transported her to this station, where both she and the baby were attended to day and night. Little Faith, then five and a half months old, was not affected, and although short of food for a time, she could not be persuaded to take artificial foods. Yet she continued to grow strong and lively and was so good tempered it seemed the blessing of God was upon her.

Colin and Mary had remained behind with Mrs Bayles, who mothered them and made them feel very much at home. Eventually another friend, Mr Johansen, from Deep Well Station fifty miles (80km) south of Alice Springs, arrived at Bloods Creek Station in his Dodge 1 ton truck. When he learned of the situation, he took Effie and the children on to Alice Springs, reaching there safely on Christmas eve. Here they were lovingly housed and cared for by Mrs Ida Standley until Erny's arrival a week later.

During his time at Bloods Creek Erny held a number of gospel services with the Indigenous people. Then finally the drought broke and rain began to fall, enabling him to start again for Alice Springs. Soon after their arrival at Bloods Creek one of their horses had died, so now his friends made him a present of two more horses, with the loan of a third for the worst part of his journey. He also had two of their first goats returned to him, after selling them to these friends two years previously, and two other young ones were given to him as well for their start in Alice Springs. He was so glad to have their little nanny again as they had received her seven years before in answer to prayer.

Finally Erny set off from Bloods Creek station with eight horses, four goats, five fowls and a cat. He was accompanied by an Aboriginal and his two chidren. The man was going to work for Erny for half the trip, then try to find his runaway wife.

All went well until they reached the Finke River, which was now in flood. Its turbulent brown waters were a quarter of a mile (1/2km) wide, with the added threat of quicksand in places. They started across, but suddenly the horses got into quicksand and lost their footing. In their panic they became tangled in their harness, then to Erny's horror, the van began sinking farther down into the water. The Aborigine had injured his leg, but managed to get himself and his children safely across.

Praying desperately, Erny plunged into the water and managed to free the horses one by one and get them across onto dry land. The poor fowls under the van just escaped drowning. He finally got them and the goats safely to land, but to rescue the van he had to send the Aborigine to the nearest station for help. When the station owner arrived he brought a wire rope, two old Aborigines and a girl who plunged into the water and carried back on her head the most valuable goods from the van.

Erny and his new friend, with the wire rope and four horses, eventually succeeded in pulling the caravan onto dry land. Then they harnessed up the six horses and pulled right through to the north bank just in time to escape a tremendous flood which would have swept the van away.

Erny and his Aboriginal friends spent Christmas Day on the road. Their dinner was damper and jam and a quart pot of tea with goat's milk in it. The Aborigine was fortunate enough to catch a goanna which he and his children roasted on the coals. He said, 'All same chicken.' So apparently his Christmas dinner was also complete.

The journey improved after that, with interludes along the way to share the gospel with small groups of Aborigines whose faces brightened when they saw Erny. They informed him that, 'a big mob wait alonga you at Alice Springs.'

At last, on the 1st January, 1924, Erny reached his destination and gave Effie and the children a happy surprise, arriving a day earlier than anticipated. He rejoiced to see Effie and the children looking so well and was extremely grateful for Mrs Standley's kindness to them all. She had truly been a 'mother of love', even though her hands were so full and her time fully occupied with her many duties as matron to the fifty half-castes in the Bungalow, as well as teaching school.

Chapter 13

A NEW HOME

On the 2nd January Erny and the family moved into the old blue-stone police barracks 2 miles (3km) out of town down through the Gap, having received kind permission to use it until their own home was erected. It needed a bit of cleaning but provided a welcome home for them for their first six months in Alice Springs.

On the first Sunday in the new year they held a thanksgiving service under the gum trees with 162 Aboriginals present, all with smiles and outstretched hands for a hearty handshake to welcome them back. They said, "Me no more sorry longa you now, me all day glad, you sit down all day, me learn'm good fellow." Erny and Effie's hearts rejoiced and echoed the words, "And the toils of the road will seem nothing, when we get to the end of the way."

The Indigenous people who had learnt some hymns from them previously assisted in the singing. But the chief leaders were Aborigines from the Lutheran Mission Station at Hermannsburg, 90 miles (144km) away, who were visiting Alice Springs at Christmas time. These dear people sang the hymns with great fervour in the Aranda tongue, so that voices in several languages blended in praise to God.

It was a memorable scene of a congregation of Aborigines under the dome of heaven in Central Australia, giving praise to the Creator and worshipping with a sincerity and reverence which could not be surpassed in any of the grand cathedrals in the capitals of the world. It was a wonderful welcome and an augury of what was yet to be accomplished among the tribes in the interior of that vast continent, by the grace and power of Jesus Christ.

Prior to leaving Melbourne, Erny had been successful in leasing from the Federal Government four blocks of land on the corners of Railway Terrace, Gregory Terrace and Bath Street, measuring approximately two acres in all. Here he was planning to build a church and a more substantial home than the canvas tents they had been living in for much of the previous ten years.

Alice Springs was built along the Todd River, but Erny's land was situated on the south-west corner, two miles (3km) out of the main town and furthest away from the river. This area was utterly barren, devoid of grass or bushes of any kind. The acacia trees that were there had been eaten down by various animals until they were just stumps. In the background rose Mt Gillen, named after an early explorer, Francis James Gillen, a telegraph operator with the Overland Telegraph Service in Alice Springs for some 25 years.

Before commencing any work on their property, Erny, Effie and the two children joined hands and prayed that God would use this land, the church and home they planned to build on it for His glory and the blessing of His people both white and Indigenous.

Then, although the weather was still extremely hot, Erny felt he should begin building and steadily worked the team of horses while the feed was good and the water plentiful. With the help of some local Aborigines he cut 360 posts and rails and 2500 stubs and carted them five to ten miles (8-16km) back to their property.

First he erected a unique rabbit-proof fence around the perimeter of the four blocks consisting of 2'6" (75cm) mulga posts hammered in close together, one of many firsts for the town.

Once the land was fenced, Erny pegged out the site for their new home. Then began the task of making bricks. Erny's experience as a brick layer's labourer stood him in good stead now as he fashioned the bricks out of sand from the Todd River and lime burnt in a home-made kiln just outside Heavitree Gap. The 6" x 6" x 12" (15x15x30cm) bricks were then left to sun-bake alongside the spot where their home was being built.

Erny built his home in a different style from others in Alice Springs.

The main framework was constructed of pines taken from Pine Gap, because of their ant resistant qualities. These had to be axed then adzed by hand, as no saw-mill was available. Erny's main Aboriginal helper, Mickey Dow-Dow, was an expert with the adze and did a commendable job.

Once the framework was up the bricks were then laid in place. The cement Erny had ordered from Port Augusta had to be hauled by camel from the terminus at Oodnadatta at a cost of 35/- ($3.50) per bag and was therefore used sparingly. All mortar was mixed by hand with Erny's only helpers being Aboriginal men from Alice Springs,

In fact, the white population of Alice Springs ridiculed the idea of building with bricks. The local police officer, Sergeant Robert Stott, even went so far as to kick at several bricks to see if they would hold together. But in time both government and private builders followed Erny's example and quite a number of brick buildings began appearing in Alice Springs.

Erny had recently received a small legacy left by his mother. With it he ordered roofing iron from Port Augusta, which was also brought by camel from the rail head at Oodnadatta. Once this was in place, Erny created ceilings from hessian wheat and potato sacks sewn together and tacked into place. These were then whitewashed with lime, as were the 6" (15cm) thick brick walls. To help cool the house, Erny put flywire insets in the walls at ground level to let in cool air and at the top to let the hot air out.

While in Port Augusta, Erny had bought several large drapery cases to pack their belongings into. With no planed wood available, Erny took these packing cases apart and from them fashioned the doors and window frames for their house.

Due to the intense heat during the day, Erny and his men worked late into the nights using kerosene lanterns. However, to save Erny, Colin and Mary travelling the two miles to school each day from The Gap, once the kitchen and family room were erected they moved in on Effie's birthday, 18th July, using two tents for sleeping quarters.

One of their first needs now was a good water supply, but being some distance from the river, the well Erny dug was 30ft (10m) deep. All wells in Alice Springs had windlasses fitted to haul the water to the top, but in time Erny went one better and installed the first windmill and three 4ft (1.2m) 400 gallon tanks so he could pipe water directly to the kitchen and bathroom. Under the tanks he built a tar-lined swimming pool 12ft wide by 4ft deep (4m x 1.2m) which was filled with the overflow from the tanks and used as a supply of water for the garden as well as for the enjoyment of the children.

Once settled in their new home, just west of the police station, eleven year old Colin and six year old Mary were able to walk quite easily to the school run by Mrs Ida Standley in a room behind the police station opposite the jail. White children had four hours' tuition from 8.00am to 12 noon. In the afternoon half-caste children received one and a half hours' schooling from 1.00pm to 2.30pm. Full-blood Aboriginal children were not allowed to attend. Thirteen-month-old Faith was toddling around happily now, playing with her dolls and always on the go, just like her father.

During all this building activity the spiritual work was not neglected. Every Sunday they had camp meetings and taught the half-caste children in Sunday School with Mrs Standley. Each Sunday night the Aborigines would gather in crowds at their place for prayer and exhortation and an enthusiastic time of singing.

At one of the camps they visited a young, full-blood woman named Miriam seemed to be listening intently to the message of God's love and forgiveness. She had been married off to an old man while quite young, but at that time she was also living with a white man of bad repute.

On their next visit they heard the old man had died, but that Miriam was still living with the white man. That day, after again hearing the message, Miriam opened her heart to the Lord and was wonderfully converted. She told Erny and Effie that now that she had Jesus in her heart she didn't want to live with the white man any more.

Shortly afterwards, Erny heard that, under the influence of drink, this man had told some white friends how very much he had loved 'that little black gin', but that now the missionaries had ruined her.

To help Miriam get away from this man's influence, Erny built her a little wurley on their property and she became a great help and companion to Effie, especially when Erny was away on his trips. Miriam found it hard to understand some of the white man's ways of doing things, but what she could understand, she did to the best of her ability. She was no good at sewing, but in time she managed to knit herself a coloured jumper. When her friends saw her wearing it they were most impressed. Miriam proudly reported back to Effie that she was the first Aboriginal woman in Alice

Springs who had ever knitted herself a jumper.

Miriam was also a great help to Effie in training other Aborigines to help around the property. Effie quickly learned that they needed to be treated firmly but kindly.

By now the heat was with them again, and it was time to prepare for their first Christmas with the Aborigines. They started with an early morning service which was very well attended. A few days previously, the mail service had delivered two new petrol cases packed full of food and gifts from friends in Adelaide, both for themselves and for the Aborigines, along with other parcels from home, all of which added to the excitement of the day for everyone.

Once the weather cooled Erny commenced building again. Wood had to be cut, hauled and prepared, and more bricks made and lime burnt. Before long, Erny was able to build a front room and bedroom across the front, with a verandah around three sides of the house. From the two Christmas petrol cases, he fashioned a couch for the front room.

With the house now basically completed, Erny dug a cellar underneath for storage and also to provide a cool dining room for extremely hot days. Later, he erected a flywire sleepout on top of the house so the girls could catch the cool night air. In time he built a swing for the children and surfaced a tennis court with crushed ant hills smoothed out with a roller pulled by a camel.

With the house under way, Erny marked out the garden. But the soil was hard clay and with the help of several Aborigines he dug out three feet (1m) of soil and replaced it with river sand mixed with manure. However, due to the drought, their first plants withered away and it was a year or so before they received much return for their hard work.

Airy Upper Room for Cool Summer Sleeping

Swing in Garden of Completed House

Chapter 14

CAMEL TREKKING

During Erny and Effie's first year at Alice Springs, 1924, there was a severe drought with no rain at all for the first ten months, and only 2.5 inches (3cm) of rain for the entire year. Feed became so scarce that by the end of the year all eight of their horses had died. This was a great blow to Erny, who had tended them lovingly, and he wondered how his dream of taking the gospel throughout the Red Centre of Australia was now to be fulfilled.

Around this time, the government decided to change the Oodnadatta-Alice Springs mail run from camels to Reo trucks. This cut the mail run from three weeks to three days. It also meant the government had quite a number of sturdy camels for sale. After watching Erny's ministry amongst the Aboriginal people with interest over the past twelve years, the Aborigines Friends Association had recently appointed Erny as their representative in Alice Springs, giving him a small regular wage. Erny now approached them about buying several of the camels and they agreed to meet the purchase price for the best five camels, plus the necessary travelling gear to go with them.

Erny fenced off a section of his property for the camels and trained the two most cooperative ones to pull his buggy. Another, named Rocket, became Erny's personal riding camel. The acquisition of these camels now opened up the possibility of new fields of service, as they were able to plod through country the horses could never have tackled, and could go for seven to fourteen days without water.

Before leaving Adelaide, Erny had also been accepted by the British and Foreign Bible Society as their representative in Alice Springs. Along with a goodly supply of Bibles and other Christian materials, Erny was allotted a small retainer for his services. Thus, along with gifts from friends down south, they were able to cover their own living expenses and also welcome many other Christians passing through Alice Springs into their home.

Erny employed an Aboriginal boy named Barney to care for the camels, and once the cooler weather arrived, Erny and Barney did a short trip to the Hermannsburg Mission Station to get the feel for the animals. They stayed there for four weeks while Erny worked on improving his knowledge of the Aranda language. Erny had been saddened to learn earlier that his good friend, Pastor Carl Strehlow, had died on the 20th October 1922 after twenty-eight years of ministry at Hermannsburg. But Mr Heinrich, who was managing the station until a replacement pastor could be found, made Erny very welcome.

While at Hermannsburg, Erny was introduced to a young Aboriginal man by the name of Albert Namatjira. Born at the mission on the 28th July 1902, Albert was already showing talent as a painter, but after receiving tuition from retired soldier and artist Rex Battarbee, a few years later his gift blossomed. In 1936, at the age of thirty-four, Albert Namatjira sold his first painting, his success leading to the emergence of a whole school of Aboriginal artists. However, Erny had the privilege of encouraging the young man and sharing special times of prayer with him long before he became famous.

Soon after Erny's return to Alice Springs he persuaded his assistant, Mickey Dow-Dow, to travel with him as his Aranda-speaking interpreter. After loading the camels with Bibles, Christian literature, medicines, flour, sugar and tea, as well as extra clothing to meet the needs of people along the way, the three men set off to take the gospel to the Aborigines further out.

Erny found that the gramophone, playing records like *Jesus Loves Me, This I Know*, and the magic lantern, showing slides of Bible stories, were a great help in bringing the message of the cross home to the hearts of the Indigenous people. He had realised early on that there was no point in teaching finer points of doctrine to the Aborigines. Many of them could not speak English at all, and he could not speak their language well enough at this stage. What he did through an interpreter was to teach them about Jesus, the love of God, and that He was the only one who could do away with sin and superstition.

On one trip they travelled toward Central Mount Stuart, the actual centre of Australia, named after explorer, John McDouall Stuart. As they plodded along between spinifex and rough undergrowth and over rocky hillocks, they carefully scanned the ground for the footmarks of wandering nomads. Suddenly, on the horizon, as the sun was lowering toward the western sky, they sighted a group of Aboriginal spearmen in full battle formation coming towards the intruders.

Erny called out to the team of camels to halt and Barney yelled, 'Hooshta,' causing the camels to drop to their knees in typical fashion. Then Mickey, Erny's trusted interpreter, advanced deftly on foot while keeping a wary eye on the poised spears. Indicating that he was unarmed, Mickey then spoke by sign language, patting the ground several times with the palms of his hands. Gradually the spears and weapons were dropped to the ground and a group of elders cautiously moved forward to greet this unknown tribesman who had indicated the peaceful mission of his white friend.

That night, under the dome of Central Australia's starry vault, these Aboriginals watched, amazed, as the magic lantern showed them pictures of the first Christmas when the Son of God came to earth as a tiny baby and the angels' song of peace and goodwill among men was first sung. That evening seeds were sown in many hearts that were to bear much fruit in times to come.

In late June 1925 Erny was back in Alice Springs when Presbyterian minister, Reverend John Flynn, superintendent of the Australian Inland Mission, and returned soldier radio technician, Mr George Towns chugged into town in their specially designed Dodge Buckboard. The two men had driven from Adelaide via Beltana, Innamincka, Birdsville, Marree and Oodnadatta, conducting inland radio transmission tests as they travelled, using a pulley drive from the jacked-up back wheel to generate electricity for their radio transmissions.

Erny was intrigued, and invited John Flynn to their home for a visit. The two men felt an immediate rapport as they discussed their shared vision to bring the gospel and medical aid to both Aboriginal and white people isolated in the far flung areas of Australia's outback.

When visiting Oodnadatta and Beltana over the years Erny had been impressed with the selfless work of the nursing sisters and padres at the Australian Inland Mission hostels. The first AIM hostel was built at Oodnadatta in 1911, with Beltana following in 1919. Flynn told Erny how he had worked over the years since to set up nursing hostels in remote areas of Western Australia, Queensland and the Northern Territory.

Although there were two AIM nursing sisters in Alice Springs, they lacked a suitable hostel and that day Flynn shared with Erny his vision to erect a strong stone building for the town with an operating theatre, airy wards and wide verandahs. He had already purchased land on Todd Street and was hoping to start negotiations for the building during this visit.

That afternoon Flynn looked over Erny's almost completed home with interest. He was particularly taken with Erny's idea of having ventilation areas at the top and bottom of his walls, and decided to use the same idea in his new hostel.

Flynn also shared with Erny his dream of eventually linking those in the outback with a Flying Doctor network. His desire was to furnish people in remote areas with a pedal wireless so they could call strategic centres like Alice Springs in a medical emergency. The centre would assess the urgency of the need and, where applicable, contact the Flying Doctor, who could reach the patient in a fraction of the time it would take by any other means.

The two men parted the best of friends, each inspired by the other's vision for the people of the outback.

The Ebenezer Church

Chapter 15

NEW BEGINNINGS

Reverend John Flynn spent most of 1926 at Alice Springs supervising the building of his new AIM hostel. It was to be called Adelaide House in appreciation of the support received from many people in Adelaide. It would be a central hub for the Flying Doctor service in the Northern Territory and he was trying out a number of innovative ideas in its erection.

Flynn had hoped to have a special ward at the back of the hostel where full-blood Aborigines could be tended by the nursing sisters. However, the townspeople objected to having Indigenous people treated at the same facility as themselves, and eventually Flynn bowed to public pressure. He did assure Erny though that the sisters would provide whatever assistance he needed in attending to the Aborgines who came to him for help.

Once the hostel was completed, Flynn persuaded Alfred Traeger, whom he had met in Adelaide, to come to Alice Springs and conduct further experiments with the pedal wireless. This time they used a 5hp Lister engine to generate power at the nursing home base and heavy copper-oxide batteries at both Hermannsburg and Arltunga. In November 1926 there was great excitement when Flynn and Traeger sent the first telegram by field radio in Australia from the engine room at the rear of Adelaide House to Hermannsburg.

While Erny was away on his camel safaris, Effie conducted the Sunday services and taught Sunday School with Mrs Standley. Through the week she held a sewing and knitting class with devotions for half-caste women. She also manned the Bible Society depot and attended to the medical needs of

Aboriginals who came to her for help, while also keeping the home running.

Erny was off on another trip in April 1926 when the new Lutheran pastor, Frederich Albrecht, and his bride, Minna, arrived in Alice Springs on their way to the Hermannsburg Mission. Effie gladly put them up for the night and the three had a special time of sharing about the things of God and their desire to bring the message of His love to the Aboriginal people of Central Australia.

For the past few days Effie and Miriam had been watching over a Christian Aboriginal woman who was close to death. As Effie and the Albrechts sat at breakfast the woman's son came running to tell Effie his mother's breath had gone. Effie asked Pastor Albrecht if he would take the funeral service and he kindly agreed. However, when they reached the camp, they found the woman was breathing again, although just barely. The Albrechts had to leave then to continue their journey, but within a short time the woman finally breathed her last.

The son asked Effie if she would use her little cart to transport his mother's body the two and a half miles (4km) to the burial ground. Once there, the group of mourners sang one hymn in English and one in Aranda. Then Effie read the verses from Ecclesiastes stating that there is a time to live and a time to die. After this she prayed for the family and thanked God for the life of the departed one. When she finished, an Indigenous Christian lad offered a moving prayer which touched the hearts of those gathered. The presence of God was very real at that moment and there was no sign of the usual wailing and distress seen at most Aboriginal funerals. Effie again thanked God for the peace, hope and security the gospel message had brought to these dear people.

Early in 1926, Effie had become aware that another litttle one would be joining their family later that year and she was overjoyed to think that this time she would be in her own home for the birth, rather than in a tent somewhere. The two AIM nurses, Sisters Pope and Small, both triple-certificated nurses, were at Effie's home for afternoon tea when she told them her news and they considered the nursing hostel should be finished in good time for the birth.

Around this time another influenza epidemic swept through the town, and the outlying Aborigines suffered badly from it. Erny was still away, and while attending to them Effie herself went down with it. One of the sisters was visiting Effie when she said, 'I am afraid we will have to come to you for the birth as our hostel will not be ready in time.'

Effie was quite happy about this, but she continued to be so weak from the effects of the influenza that she wondered how she was going to get through the birth. She prayed for a quick and painless delivery and God heard. Erny was back home when, on the 28th August 1926, little Grace Murchison arrived to complete the Kramer family. It was a miracle which even astonished the sisters, who claimed it was the most wonderful birth they had ever attended, everything went so perfectly.

One of the nurses tended Effie and the baby for two weeks before leaving them to Erny's tender care. But even with Miriam's help, Erny also had to care for the other three children, run the home, and keep up with all his own work, plus the Sunday services, and he was becoming quite exhausted. Effie was very concerned for him and prayed that God would provide someone else to help them. Their kind neighbours, 50 miles (80km) away, heard of their plight and sent their eldest daughter, to come and stay with them for four weeks. She was marvellous at caring for Effie and little Grace, as well as managing the household. It was as if a great weight rolled off Erny, and he returned to his own work with renewed vigour.

One deep disappointment to Effie though was that, being so thin and weak from the influenza, she was not able to feed little Grace herself. Instead, the baby was reared on goat's milk, and to everyone's relief, she thrived. When the first lass was needed back home, her younger sister came and stayed with them for three months, and they greatly appreciated her help and company.

To Effie's disappointment, though, she took more than seven months to put on weight and recover her strength, which meant even ordinary tasks were quite a challenge.

Erny had already started to gather timber and make bricks to build the first church in Alice Springs, one especially for Aboriginal people. Now that he was freed up to work on the church again, he and his Aboriginal helpers put their hearts into it. Before long they had the basic structure up, with a medical dispensary and store at one end. Two wings of the church were built of bricks, with brush work around the rest of the building, and a trim bough and thatch roof on it. Erny named the church Ebenezer Tabernacle, meaning, 'Hitherto has the Lord helped us', from 1 Samuel 7:12.

Teddy, Miriam and Mickey making damper

On Christmas morning, 1926, they had a decorated Christmas tree for their first Christmas service in the church. With 300 Aborigines seated on the white sandy floor they shared an uplifting time of singing, worship and the retelling of the Christmas story. That night they had another service in the church, again with around 300 Aboriginal folk present, and great blessing on the service. At the close of the service Erny told the people to come back at 'piccaninny daylight' the following day for a special Christmas programme. The Aborigines took him at his word and began arriving at 4.30am the next morning!

Erny organised various games and sports for the young folks, with prizes for the winners. Then, with the help of Miriam and another Aboriginal woman, Effie treated everyone, including the aged, the blind and the lame to a Christmas dinner, not of turkey and plum pudding, but of curried goat-meat stew and damper, with a quart pot of tea each which everyone heartily enjoyed.

Erny and Effie had received support from the AFA and Adelaide friends for the Aborigines' Christmas treat and Effie and Miriam had made several big tins of bush biscuits with plenty of fruit in them. They had also made up packets of sweets for the children.

Even three-and-a-half year old Faith joined in handing out the sweets to the Aboriginal children. When all the activities were finished they gave everyone something to take back to their camps for their next meal and everyone went away happy. All in all it had been a very successful Christmas programme, one which they hoped to repeat in the years to come.

Chapter 16

CHANGES

Once the weather was cool enough, early in May 1927 Erny set off on a patrol with Pastor Albrecht, who was now fluent in the Aranda language, and a team of Aboriginal men from Hermannsburg Mission. Erny's desire was to be able to speak Aranda well enough to preach to the people directly, or at least converse with them in their own tongue about their everyday needs and problems.

Erny had a great respect for Pastor Albrecht, and the two men had a further bond, being able to converse with one another in German as well as English or Aranda. Born in a German Lutheran community near the Polish border in 1894, Friedrich Albrecht had a childhood accident which left him with a permanent limp, causing him to walk with a stick. Desiring to become a missionary, Friedrich had begun training at Hermannsburg Seminary, Hannover, Germany, when World War I broke out.

He became a Red Cross stretcher bearer, serving in France and on the Russian border. Early in the war, his parents, sisters and brothers were taken in rail trucks to Siberia, where an outbreak of cholera led to the deaths of five members of his family. Albrecht was awarded the Iron Cross for bravery in rescuing a man while under fire. Medical knowledge gained in the trenches helped him to later treat sickness and accidents at Hermannsburg Mission in Central Australia.

After the war Albrecht completed his theological training at Hermannsburg, Germany and was appointed to the Hermannsburg Mission in Australia. But first he went to a Lutheran Seminary at Dubuque, Iowa, USA to become fluent in English. His fiancee, Minna Gevers, followed him to Winnipeg, Canada, where they were married before sailing for Australia.

At Hermannsburg, a blind Aborigine named Moses gave Pastor Albrecht daily lessons in his native tongue and within nine months the pastor was fluent enough to take the whole service in Aranda without an interpreter. Minna Albrecht quickly endeared herself to the Aboriginal women by her kind and gentle ways, as she cared for them and their children. In time the Albrechts had five children: Helene, Theodor, Paul, Minna and Martin. Through the years, they all remained close friends with the Kramer family, Helene, especially, becoming a close friend of the Kramer girls.

On his return from the trip with Pastor Albrecht, Erny knew difficult family changes were looming. Colin and Mary had happily attended Mrs Standley's school for the past three years without missing one day through sickness. At the end of 1926, Colin and two other children were the first to sit for the Grade 7 Qualifying Certificate and all passed with flying colours. Colin was now fourteen, and Erny and Effie knew that before long he would need to go south to learn a trade. But they could not afford the trip just then and Mrs Standley agreed to let him attend school for another six months.

Colin had always been a cheerful and industrious young man, trying his hand at any task that arose, whether it be gardening, saddle work, mending shoes or preparing cool drinks for the family in summer. Effie knew she would miss him dearly, especially when Erny was away. It had also been a comfort to Erny knowing Colin was there to help Effie with any problems that arose. One day Colin said to her, 'I don't know how Dad is going to manage without me, Mum.' Effie replied, 'I don't know either, my lad.' But they all knew that, for Colin's sake, they had to be prepared for the parting.

Finally, by mid-September enough funds had come in for Effie to begin planning seriously for the trip south. Apart from the need for Colin to find employment, Effie knew that, for her own health, she needed a break from the heat and stress of the work in Alice Springs. It would also be an opportunity to take four-year-old Faith and thirteen-month-old Grace to Victoria to meet her family.

The morning of their departure came. Effie was going away with three of the family and leaving Mary, not yet ten, to look after her Daddy. The

Aborigines were all around them crying and showing their sorrow at Colin going away. As Erny kissed him goodbye and helped him into the car, his voice gave way as he said, 'Good-bye and God bless you my son.'

They travelled the 350 miles (560km) to the railhead at Oodnadatta in the mail truck. Then came the long train journey to Adelaide. A Presbyterian minister, who had visited them in Alice Springs the previous year, had taken a special interest in Colin and now gave him a letter of introduction to a Mr Perry. This man agreed to put Colin to work in the store room at his factory for twelve months, then, if Colin still wanted to work with tools, Mr Perry promised he would give him an apprenticeship and send him to the School of Mines to be trained. It was a wonderful answer to their prayers.

Colin continued to work there for over seven years, and left with a first class certificate as a boiler maker. What was more important to his loving parents was that, with over 400 men in that factory, during these years Colin managed to withstand all temptations and was quite involved in church, Christian Endeavour and Sunday School activities, as well as singing in the choir, as he sought to live daily for his Lord.

Once Colin was settled, Effie took Faith and Grace and travelled the 570 miles (912km) by rail to Victoria to spend time with her family. She hadn't realised just how exhausted she was until the two little girls were in good hands and she could just relax and give in to herself. Although Effie didn't know it at the time, this was to be the last time she saw her dear mother on earth, so the memories of this visit were to remain with Effie in later years as especially precious ones.

It was three months before Effie felt strong enough to return to Alice Springs and during this time, on the 9th January 1928, Mary celebrated her tenth birthday. Although the family were overjoyed to be reunited once more, Colin's empty chair tugged at all their hearts. However, once the weather was cool enough, Erny and his two helpers set out again to visit a number of camps to the north of Alice Springs.

They were back in town again when Erny heard the news that Reverend John Flynn's dream had finally become a reality. On the 17th May 1928, Dr K St Vincent Welch, with pilot Arthur Affleck at the controls of *Victory,* had answered the first call received at Cloncurry, Queensland, by the AIM Aerial Medical Service – later to be known as the Royal Flying Doctor Service – and a new era of outback care had begun.

Chapter 17

DEVELOPMENTS

For some time the Aborigines Friends Association had wanted to ascertain more clearly the needs and population of the Aborigines in the interior of Australia. So in early June a Mr J Huston Edgar arrived in Alice Springs to accompany Erny on a trip of research and discovery. They would be traversing wide expanses of barren desert and would need to cover their own needs for food and water, as well as having supplies to distribute to needy Aborigines along the way. With this in mind, Erny obtained a sixth camel, and each was fully laden with supplies to meet every conceivable emergency, including thirty gallons of water.

On the 11th June 1928 they set out with Barney as interpreter, as Mickey had gone walkabout. Travelling south-west, via Owen Springs and Henbury Station, they arrived at Erldunda Station, where they replenished their water and meat supplies before setting off into the uncivilised wilds of Central Australia. This area was officially regarded as unsafe for travellers, with earlier expeditions suffering the loss of one or more of their number to native spears. But Erny and Mr Edgar had committed their venture to God and looked to Him to guide and protect them.

Various springs and wells along the way proved to be dry and it was not until they reached Mt Conner that they found enough water to fill even one water bag. Moving on south past Kelly Hills, they finally arrived at a fine water supply in the Western Musgrave Ranges known as

Opperinna Springs, 320 miles (512km) from Alice Springs. They had seen no Indigenous people so far on their travels, but now they caught a glimpse of smoke and discovered a group of ten nomadic Aborigines.

They were informed that this area, belonging to the Pitjantjarra people, was at present deserted, owing to a recent death in the tribe.

Three days later they caught up with a group of thirty seven Opperinna Aborigines to whom they gave sweets, flour and other rations, as well as attending to a sick man. That evening Erny showed slides on the life of Christ with Barney interpreting. Next morning Annee, the Chief of Opperinna, offered to accompany them on their journey to help them find water and also to make safe contact with other Indigenous people. A hunter named Monjala also joined their party and showed his skill in catching a number of rabbits for food.

At Lake Wilson they found good water before moving on to Strawbridge Springs, where they discovered more water and a veritable oasis of feed for the camels. Leaving the pack camels with Barney and Annee so they could rest and recover their strength, Erny, Mr Edgar and the hunter set out on riding camels to travel a further thirty miles into Western Australia. They reached Harriet Springs on 11th July 1928, having travelled 480 miles (752km) in the thirty days since leaving Alice Springs. From the western end of Mt Hinckley they had the interesting experience of enjoying a clear view across the corner where the three states met.

Returning to Strawbridge Springs the party then retraced their way back to Mt Mann. Here they were met by a group of Aborigines with the men and even women highly armed and menacing. All were completely naked, yet were not ashamed. A number of young men strode up to their camels to check them out. Annee and Monjala assured the newcomers of the good intentions of the white men, and before long a crowd of 119 men, women and children, plus numerous dogs, had gathered to curiously eye off the visitors.

Erny again handed out rations and sweets to all, which seemed to meet with their approval. That evening he showed slides on the life of Christ and, with Barney interpreting, told them simply of the love and forgiveness of God. This was a completely new experience for these people, and from time to time they burst out laughing. But this was not the worst, Erny had just started the gramophone playing when around forty tamed wild dogs in the camp all began howling along with it.

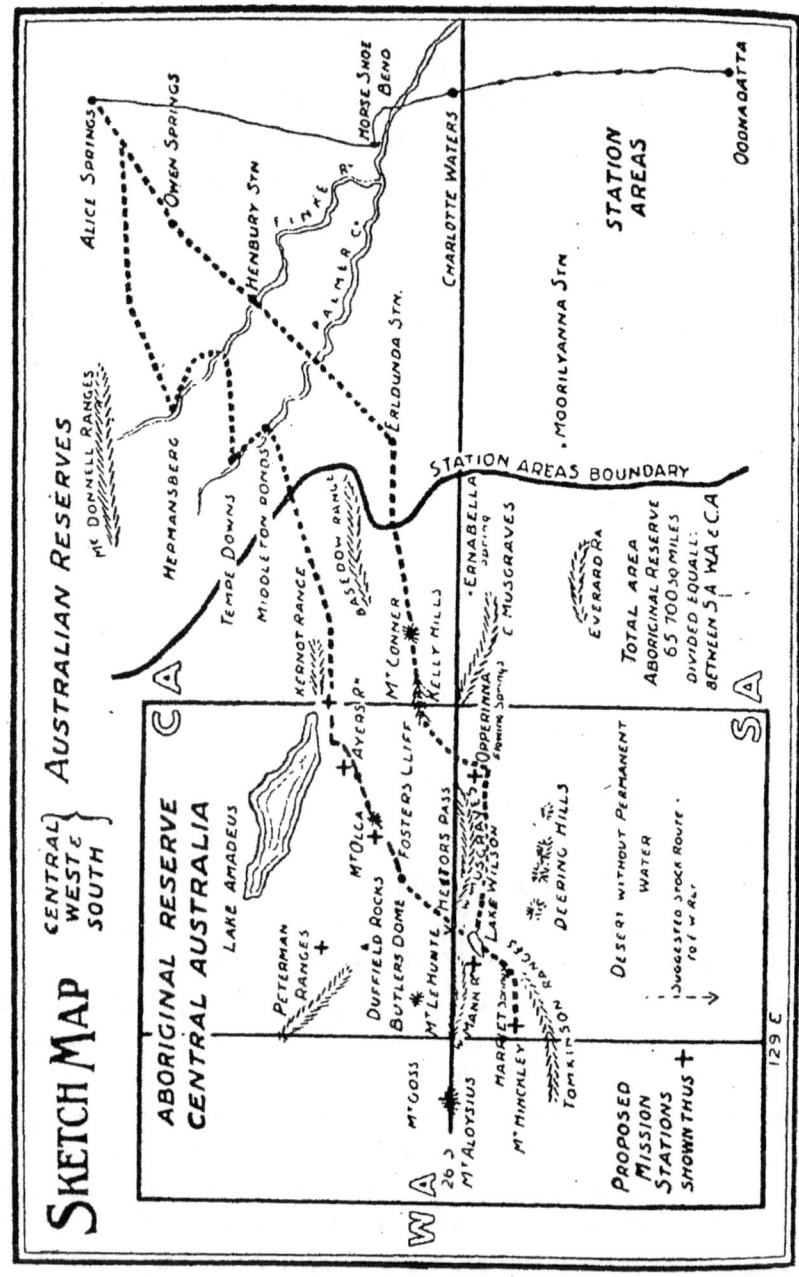

When their party started out next morning, about half the Aborigines followed them. Erny finally convinced them to go back, and when their own group reached Lake Wilson, Annee and Monjala also decided to return home. Erny loaded them up with a good supply of rations in appreciation for their help, and the two set off happily, no doubt with fascinating stories to tell of their time with the white men.

Moving on north, Erny and his party travelled through much poor country until they reached Mt Olga – or Kata-Tjuta, 'Great Old Man', to the Aboriginals. They found good water at nearby Felix Springs, then struck out due east another 20 miles (32km) to Ayer's Rock – or Uluru, meaning 'Mystery Rock' to the Aboriginals. Rising 1,142ft (348m) above the surrounding plain, this orange-hued rock was the most sacred spot in all the country around there. Here the Indigenous people came for special ceremonies, certain sections of which must not be witnessed by Aboriginal women on pain of death. A group of Indigenous people was camped near the rock when they arrived, and that night Erny again showed his slides and shared the gospel with them.

Travelling on an old Aboriginal track between the Kernott and Basedow Ranges, they eventually reached Palmer Creek. Here they were cordially welcomed by Mr Butler and were able to replenish their water supply from a fine well. Medical remedies were needed here by the Aborigines and rations were distributed to the old and sick.

Their next stop was Tempe Downs Station, after which they made for the Finke River and travelled along it for about forty miles (64km) to the Hermannsburg Mission Station, where they were warmly welcomed by Pastor Albrecht. They rested there for one day, then set out for Alice Springs, which they reached early in August, having travelled a distance of over 1000 miles (1600km) in eight weeks.

They thanked God that there had been no major disasters or confrontations, and that their need for food and water had been adequately met along the way. More importantly to Erny, seeds of the gospel had been sown among several groups of Aborigines that he prayed would bear fruit in time to come.

Soon after his return home Erny had a very interesting situation arise. Miriam had worked faithfully for Effie for over four years, and Effie had come to look on her almost as a sister. But Miriam's tribe had often commented that Miriam had no man, no children and no dog. Then one day an attractive young Christian full-blood Aborigine came to their store to get medicine for some sick friends. His name was Teddy, and soon after this Erny took him on as a permanent garden boy, a task he took to most conscientiously. Before long Teddy found himself strongly attracted to Miriam.

One day Miriam came to Erny and said, 'Me want to talk longa you, Mr Kramer.' Erny said, 'Well Miriam, what is it you want to say to me?' Miriam replied, 'Me likem Teddy and Teddy likem me.' Erny said, 'Well I'm very glad, I like to hear of two young people liking one another. Now if you be two good young fellows, when Christmas time come up I marry you.'

So they kept true and faithful to one another for nearly three months. Then one evening, just before Christmas, they had a special double wedding with a half-caste couple in the church. Effie had made Miriam a special wedding dress out of white calico, and provided a tasty wedding supper with cakes, dates, sweets and cocoa. After a walkabout honeymoon, the two lived happily in the little one room hut Erny had built for them

in his garden. Miriam continued helping Effie in the house while Teddy worked faithfully in the garden.

Teddy became a good, trustworthy young helper around the place. Each Wednesday while Erny was away, Effie would send Teddy one way and Miriam another to go and visit the people in the various camps outside of town and let her know of any who were sick.

There was one rather unruly half-caste man who had a hop beer shop where the Aborigines used to congregate. The police were anxious to catch these idle

Aboriginals, who were not allowed by law to drink alcohol. Unfortunately, one Wednesday Teddy had been doing his rounds for Effie and had just called at this particular camp intending to get another boy to go with him to the other camps. When the patrol came along and asked him what he was doing there, Teddy said Mrs Kramer had sent him there. The police, not knowing the boy, thought he was lying, particularly as he had money in his pocket, and they ordered him to get into their truck.

That evening, when Miriam came home she told Effie with a very sad heart that her Teddy was in jail. Effie exclaimed, 'In jail! Whatever for?' When the police called on Effie she assured them Teddy was honest and trustworthy and it was just unfortunate that he was found on those premises at that time with money in his pocket which she had indeed given him. She told them she was depending on Teddy to help her with domestic duties. After they left, Miriam began sobbing so inconsolably that soon Mary and Faith were weeping brokenheartedly with her. Effie decided it was time to turn things around and she gathered the three girls to her and in heartfelt prayer she placed the whole situation in the Lord's loving hands.

The next morning around 10.00am Teddy suddenly appeared, all smiles. He said he hadn't slept all night but kept praying for them all, just like Paul and Silas had when they were thrown into prison. Within a very short time Teddy's friends and relatives had all gathered round to shake his hand and welcome him back, almost as if he had returned from the dead.

Effie trusted Teddy and Miriam implicitly. Often when she and Erny were away for a few days they would leave Teddy and Miriam in charge. When they returned the home would be spotless with everything in place. If Miriam knew when to expect them she would also have the kettle boiling and the table laid for a meal.

The idea of going walkabout was deeply embedded in the Aboriginal psyche, and Teddy and Miriam were no different. Yet Effie worked out with them that they could go on two walkabouts each year, providing they let her know in advance so she could have other helpers arranged for that time. This worked well for both parties, and they never let her down. But their replacements were another matter.

Effie had been spoilt with two such good and honest workers, so it was hard when she found her new helpers stealing and lying to her. It was especially difficult for Effie to get any Aboriginal man to obey her when

Erny was away. They would take the food and clothing she provided, then go and sleep somewhere without cleaning the camel's yard, watering the garden or any other task she had assigned them. Effie was always relieved to see Teddy and Miriam return from their walkabout.

Early in 1929, Erny was appointed Protector of Aborigines, Alice Springs, by the Commonwealth Government, and was supplied with rations to distribute to those in need. In this capacity he was also asked for his opinion on various problems concerning the Indigenous population of Central Australia. His replies to the Minister for Home Affairs in Canberra, Mr C L Abbott, were given serious consideration with further correspondence entered into. In due time, many of Erny's suggestions were acted upon, to the benefit of the Indigenous population.

On another occasion Erny was asked to give evidence at a Royal Commission in Darwin on conditions amongst outback Aborigines, especially the ill-treatment of women and children. This again resulted in Erny's recommendations being heeded and official decisions being made for their good.

In 1928 Mrs Standley, the children's school teacher, had taken her fifty half-caste charges and moved out to the Jay Creek Aboriginal settlement, where she taught full-blood children as well. A Miss Burton had taken her place as teacher of the white children at Alice Springs. In March 1929, Mrs Standley had a serious heart attack, and Erny was asked by the government if he would proceed to Jay Creek immediately and supervise matters there until a replacement could be found for her. This he did, until a married couple, Mr and Mrs Thorne, arrived to relieve him, but everyone missed Mrs Standley's loving ways and cheerful presence.

However, the biggest change to affect all their lives was the arrival of the railway in Alice Springs. For months everyone had watched eagerly as the track was levelled, sleepers were laid and finally the rails bolted in place. The excitement of the town reached fever pitch as the first train chugged to the end of the line in Alice Springs at 2.00am on the 6th August 1929 having left Adelaide early on the 4th August. Early though the hour was, this was a gala occasion, and no-one wanted to miss it. As the train drew to a halt at the terminus in Railway Terrace, alongside Ebenezer Tabernacle, the waiting crowd cheered, anticipating the tremendous change for the better this would make to their every day existence.

Chapter 18

FAR AND WIDE

Over the next five years Erny continued to spend six months of each year travelling as far north as Tennant Creek, west to the Petermann Ranges, south to Oodnadatta and east to the Queensland border. With his two helpers, Barney and Mickey, Erny traversed many thousands of miles, taking the message of God's love and forgiveness to those who had never heard it. Besides their own food, water and clothing, his camels carried the magic lantern, slides, gramophone and records, as well as medical supplies and extra food for those in need.

Erny was often the first white man the Aborigines had ever seen, yet he was greatly encouraged on subsequent visits to find that those who had responded to his earlier message were still going on faithfully with the Lord. At one of Erny's camp meetings an old man named Jim enthusiastically joined in singing the various hymns and showed special interest in Erny's talk. Afterwards Erny asked him where he had first heard of God's love. He replied that it was at Eringa Station when Erny was there eleven years ago. He went on, 'Me can't loosem Boss (pointing up to heaven), me all day pray.'

Erny was happy to minister to Indigenous and white people alike. Yet in all of his travels through the outback Erny never arrived at a station homestead in an untidy state. He always stopped some distance away to shave and have a good clean up, believing the Bible teaching that cleanliness is next to godliness.

Outback Evangelist

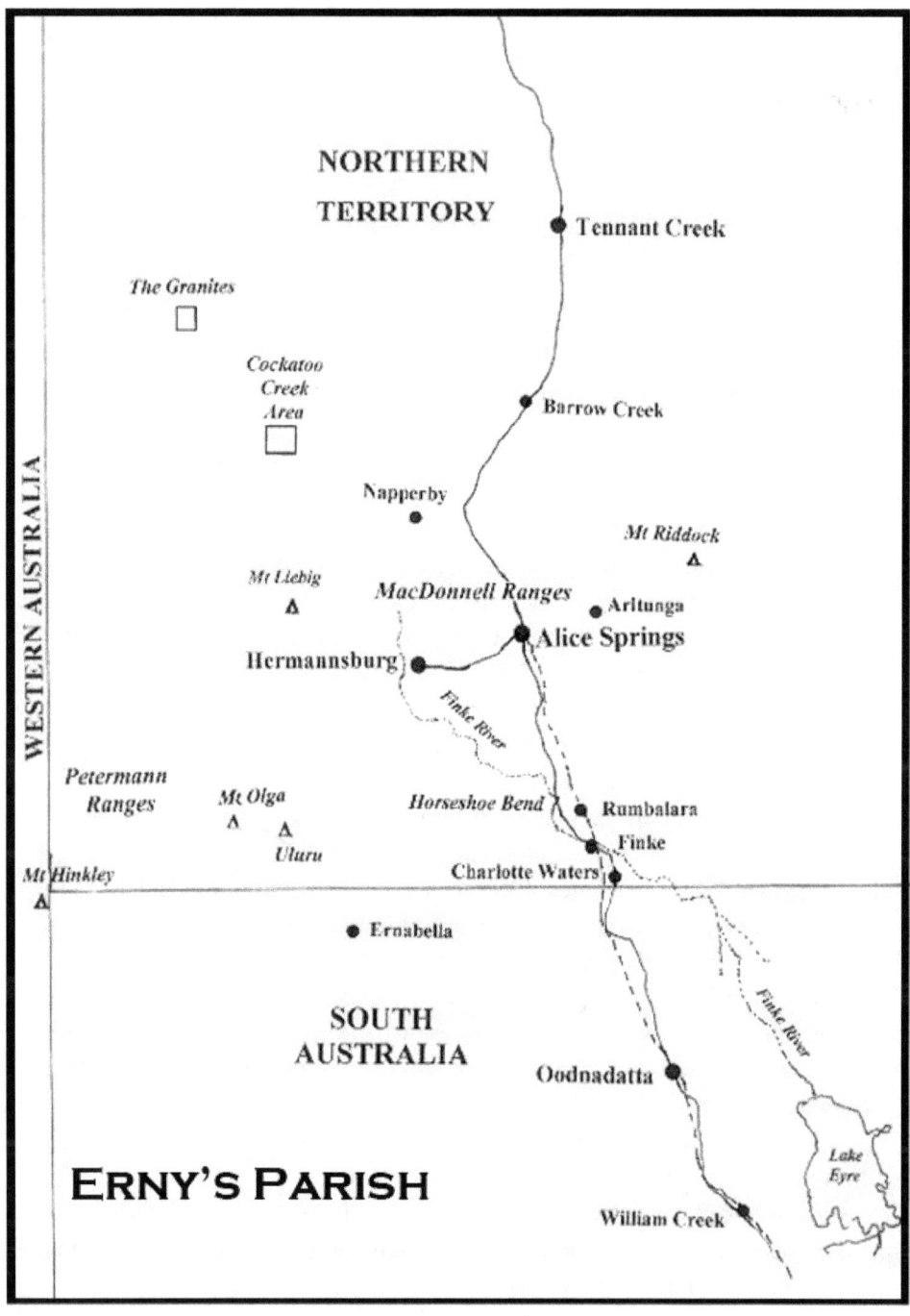

On one of these trips Erny visited the recently completed Rumbalara siding on the new railway line twenty miles (32km) north of Finke. The name Rumbalara was taken from the local Aboriginal name, Umbalara, meaning rainbow, from the gloriously hued ochre cliffs lining the nearby Finke River.

Erny was warmly welcomed by the Tindale family who excitedly told him of the visit of the Governor of South Australia, Sir Alexander Hore-Ruthven, and his wife. The governor's special carriage had been attached to the rear of a stock train for his official visit to Alice Springs. The train had stopped briefly at the siding and the Tindale family had been encouraged to come and meet the Governor and his wife. Lady Hore-Ruthven was appalled that a woman with a young family was living in such conditions, especially with no fresh milk for the children.

While in Alice Springs Lady Hore-Ruthven bought a goat for the Tindales and on the return trip the train was delayed while Lady Hore-Ruthven came and had afternoon tea at their home. Apart from the goat, she also brought them a supply of fresh bread and gave Mrs Flo Tindale one of her dresses. The family were very touched by her kindness to them. Sir Alexander Hore-Ruthven later became Governor General of Australia.

The Tindales' son, Percy, later wrote that the children found it amazing to watch the Biblical slides Erny's magic lantern had projected onto a sheet hung on the side of their house, using a carbide light. He remarked that Erny's visits were the only contact the family had with religion all through those years.

During a trip north to Barrow Creek Erny held fruitful services at stations and Aboriginal camps along the way, dispensing food, medicine and spiritual help to all in need. As he was leaving one camp the following morning, some of the older folk came to him with tears in their eyes and said, 'Please Boss, come again to see us more.' It was both an encouragement and a challenge as Erny sought to reach out to people in all directions for the Lord.

On another trip through the Western MacDonnell Ranges Erny explored the magnificent, 360ft (100m) high, brilliant red chasm known as Gall Springs, 25 miles (40km) west of Alice Springs and 5 miles (8km) north of the road to Hermannsburg. At his recommendation it was renamed Standley Chasm in honour of Mrs Ida Standley, first school teacher at Alice

Springs who taught both half-caste and white children for many years before taking her half-caste charges to the nearby Jay Creek Aboriginal settlement. She later received the MBE for her work among the Aborigines.

A frequent visitor to Erny's home during these years was Professor John Cleland. Born at Norwood, South Australia, on the 22nd June 1878, Professor Cleland was the first Marks Professor of Pathology at the University of Adelaide. He helped form the Board of Anthropological Research at the University, which he chaired for nearly thirty years.

From 1925 to 1939 Professor Cleland spent most of his summer holidays on expeditions to Central Australia conducting Indigenous Health Research. For almost ten years, while enjoying the warm hospitality of their home, Professor Cleland would discuss various Aboriginal culture and health needs with Erny.

In August 1931 Professor Cleland led a team, including Dr T D Campbell, Professor Sir Stanton Hicks and other members of the University Board of Anthropology, on a scientific health research expedition to Central Australia. Professor Cleland contacted Erny prior to leaving Adelaide, and requested his help in gathering as large a group of Aboriginals as possible at Cockatoo Creek, about 225 miles (357 km) north-west of Alice Springs.

Erny, with Barney, Mickey and their camel team, journeyed throughout the country leading to Cockatoo Creek and persuaded the various groups of Indigenous people to follow him there. Such was the confidence reposed in Erny by the Aborigines that, from Napperby Station onwards, they freely followed him until around one hundred and fifty men, women and children were assembled at Cockatoo Creek when the members of the expedition arrived.

Some of the Aborigines present had been involved in the killing of a white man a few years previously, resulting in severe retribution from white police. This made them somewhat apprehensive of these white men's intentions, but Erny stressed the peaceful nature of the expeditions' aims. He encouraged the Aborigines to trust the visitors and submit to their examinations in the interests of future help for their various health needs. Such was their trust in Erny that, without the slightest sign of antagonism on the part of any Aborigine, they submitted to blood tests and other tedious routines with the utmost goodwill and docility, proving much better subjects than most Europeans would have in like circumstances.

Never one to miss an opportunity, on the Sunday morning Erny held a Christian service in English, translated into Aranda, under the gum trees in the dry bed of Cockatoo Creek which everyone attended. In the afternoon he held a special children's service, which was enjoyed as much by the adults as the children. Then in the evening, under the starry dome of heaven, Erny showed slides on the life of Christ with his magic lantern and once more both Aborigines and white men alike heard the simple gospel message of God's love and forgiveness offered to all mankind through faith in Jesus.

After winding up their experiments a few days later, the members of the expedition expressed their heartfelt appreciation for the part Erny had played in making this one of their most successful expeditions yet. Before leaving they handed Erny a supply of surplus medical supplies, plus provisions to distribute among the Aborigines as thanks for their co-operation. This, along with the sympathetic attitude shown to the Aborigines by the Expedition members, went a long way to healing the wounds between Indigenous people and whites caused by the earlier tragedy.

On his return to Adelaide, Professor Cleland wrote a long letter of appreciation to the Aborigines Friends Association, thanking them for allowing Erny to assist with the research and outlining the great work he had done on their behalf. He wrote:

'We were daily witnesses of the confidence reposed by the natives in Mr Kramer and of the confidence he himself placed in the Aborigines. Whenever any delicate question arose or we were undecided as to what line of action to take, Mr Kramer's knowledge of the Aborigine came to our assistance and guided our actions.

'Mr Kramer's visits to all parts of Central Australia have brought him in contact with these wandering individuals and he has done as much as to us seems humanly possible to minister to their physical ailments and

to convey to them some idea of goodwill and kindness between man and man. .... We look upon him as a fearless protector of the rights of the natives and as doing as much as anyone in Australia to protect the members of this rapidly disappearing race.'

On another university expedition to Mt Liebig, 200 miles (320km) north-west of Alice Springs, for which Erny acted as guide to the same team. Max Lamshed, Adelaide Advertiser reporter with the expedition wrote,

'the (Aboriginal) people were wonderfully responsive to kindness. Much of this reaction, no doubt, is a result of the work of Mr E E Kramer, missionary of the Aborigines Friends Association among them, for they have learned from him that the white man is kind.'

Cleland Conservation Park in the Mount Lofty Ranges of South Australia was opened in Professor Cleland's honour in 1967, four years before his death in 1971.

Another frequent visitor to the Kramer home was anthropologist Ted Strehlow, (later Professor) son of Erny's late friend, pastor Carl Strehlow. Born at Alice Springs on the 6th June 1908, Theodore Strehlow had grown up at Hermannsburg Mission with a deep love and understanding of the Aranda people and their culture. Ted, as he was called, was only fourteen when his father died in Oct 1922, and he moved down to Adelaide to complete his education at the University of Adelaide.

Later, on his many visits north, often using the Kramer home as his base, Ted collected much information on Tribal Law, and revised his father's translation of the New Testament in the Aranda language. Adopted by the Aranda people as a member of their tribe, in May 1933 Ted was entrusted by their chiefs with numerous sacred artefacts, called tjurunga, as well as secrets involved in their tribal ceremonies.

Appointed a Commonwealth Patrol Officer,on a visit to the Petermann Ranges in 1936, Ted Strehlow was one of the first Europeans to make worthwhile contact with the Pitjantjatjara people. A noted linguist, lecturer and world authority on Aranda (Arrente) culture, Ted later established the Strehlow Research Foundation in Adelaide but died tragically on the day of its opening in October 1978.

In October 1988 legislation was passed to establish the Strehlow Research Centre in Alice Springs to house the Strehlow Collection.

It represented forty-five years of Ted Strehlow's anthropological and ethnological research along with films, genealogies, artefacts, sacred objects and recorded oral traditions, all meticulously recorded by him. This collection is of both national and international significance.

Many streets in Alice Springs are named after these early pioneers, including Strehlow Street, Flynn Drive, Standley Crescent and Kramer Court, just off Albrecht Drive.

In 1934 Scottish doctor, Charles Duguid, visited Erny and Effie at Alice Springs. The murder of a white man by Aborigines at Landers Creek a few years earlier had resulted in seventeen Aborigines being shot by police during the hunt for the murderer. The injustice of this had sparked Dr Duguid's interest in Aboriginal rights, and he spent many hours talking with Erny over the issue of basic rights for the Indigenous people. A year later, in 1935, Dr Duguid, with his wife Phyllis, founded the Aboriginal Advancement League with himself as president. A devout Presbyterian, in 1935 Dr Duguid was also elected Moderator of the Presbyterian Church of South Australia.

On one of Erny's visits south-west of Erldunda Station he had explored the area around Ernabella, at the eastern end of the Musgrave Range, with a view to establishing a mission station there. As he walked around the area praying for the Aborigines in the vicinity who had never known God's love, God's words in Joshua 1:3 seemed to be spoken directly to his heart, 'Every place that the sole of your foot will tread upon I have given you.' Yet at that time there was no way Erny himself could take up this promise.

During Dr Duguid's visit however, Erny shared with him the burden on his heart for a Christian mission to be established at Ernabella to reach out to the Aborigines of that area. To Erny's delight, in 1937 Dr Duguid helped found the Ernabella Aboriginal Mission in the Musgrave Ranges of South Australia as an outreach of the Presbyterian Church. The church administered the mission for 37 years before handing it over to the Ernabella Community Council on the 1st January 1974. In 1970 Dr Charles Duguid was awarded the OBE for his work among the Aborigines. He died in Adelaide on the 5th December 1986 at the age of 102, and in accordance with his wishes was buried at Ernabella.

Chapter 19

END OF THE ROAD

In late December 1933 Colin returned home after an absence of four years. There was great rejoicing as the family shared Christmas together once more. Mary's sixteenth birthday followed on the 9th January, then on the 28th January a special family party was held to celebrate Colin's twenty-first birthday.

The family in Alice Springs

Yet the happy celebrations were somewhat tinged with sadness. For some time now Mary's health had not been the best and Erny and Effie realised that she needed the benefit of life down south to help her pick up again. It was a real answer to prayer when an opportunity arose for her in the Women's Training Home at the Melbourne Bible Institute, under the supervision of the Reverend C H Nash.

So early in February 1934, Effie and Mary accompanied Colin on his return trip to Adelaide. Then they went on to Melbourne to get Mary settled into her new quarters. A brief visit out to the farm followed, but this, too, was tinged with sadness, Effie's mother having passed to her eternal reward a short time earlier. Then, after spending a few more days with Mary, Effie returned to Adelaide in time to spend Easter with Colin.

When Effie eventually reached Alice Springs after a three day train journey, she was dismayed to see how gaunt and run-down Erny had become. He had endured a particularly hot, trying summer and had missed his wife and daughter very much. There had been no rain for many months, with much resultant sickness among the Aborigines. Then, just prior to Effie's return, a serious epidemic of eye trouble had broken out in the Aboriginal camps and they had set up isolated hospitals for the white, half-caste and Indigenous people. Erny had worked long hours doing his utmost to assist the doctor and police, but his untiring efforts had taken their toll. He had no appetite and was just a shadow of his former self.

As soon as the eye trouble abated sufficiently, however, Erny made preparations to go 315 miles (506km) north to Tennant Creek where there was a gold rush. He was particularly concerned for the Aborigines of the area, especially those who had become Christians on his previous visits. But first he seized the opportunity of a quick run with a car driver out to the Granites Gold Field on the edge of the Tanami Desert, 375 miles (600km) from Alice Springs. The trip took less than one week, but it gave Erny an insight into the roughness and deadliness of the country, and also the harsh conditions to be faced in a gold mining camp.

While there, he met a Mr Chapman, and in course of conversation Erny found that Mr Chapman wanted to buy property in Alice Springs. Erny began to think seriously about their present situation. For quite a while now Erny and Effie had realised they needed to advance with the times. When they had first arrived in Alice Springs ten years previously cars were not thought of and camels were the most useful animals for the outback.

Now when the various churches sent their missionaries to the outback, they came equipped with cars, and were able to cover long distances in a relatively short time. A few years previously a neighbour returning to Adelaide had offered to let Erny have his Oakland 6 car quite cheaply, and it was gratefully accepted. But the vehicle was not sturdy enough to travel over rough outback roads, and was used mainly for short trips around Alice Springs.

After nine years of frequent travel on the none-too-comfortable back of a camel, the jolts and jerks, along with the accompanying privations and lack of good food, were beginning to tell on Erny's health and physical frame. The doctor had indicated that the only hope for an improvement in health was to give up the work in Alice Springs and return south for specialist medical treatment. Erny was loath to leave the work that had been his life and calling for the past twenty-one years, yet the indications were that this phase of his ministry was drawing to a close.

Another pointer was the nature of the work amongst the full-blood Aborigines of the area. Previously, when Erny was away for a period of up to sixteen weeks Effie would have a regular attendance of around fifty Aborigines at the church services. But with Alice Springs now expanding, the Aborigines were being pushed further and further out into the scrub lands. With so few Aborigines living within easy distance of the church they were now lucky to get eight or nine to the services.

It was not as if they would be leaving Alice Springs without a Christian witness. In 1931, while visiting Barrow Creek, Erny had met up with a fine British couple, Methodist minister, Reverend Harry Griffiths and his wife, Dorothy, who were then stationed at Katherine. On Erny's recommendation, in 1932 the Methodist Inland Mission had reappointed the Griffiths to Alice Springs and the two families had become fast friends.

Although the Methodist Church services were aimed primarily at the white population, Harry's International work truck often doubled as an ambulance and he and Dorothy gave medical and dental help, along with spiritual guidance, to the Aborigines wherever needed. In Alice Springs, Dorothy had started Guide and Brownie groups and Harry took the Scouts. In many ways the Griffiths were carrying on the caring Christian roles established by Erny and Effie over the past nine years.

With all these factors weighing on their hearts and minds, Erny and Effie gave themselves to prayer, seeking the Lord's direction for their future. However, with the needs of the Aborigines at Tennant Creek heavy on his heart, Erny loaded up the camels for one final journey. Knowing how unfit he was for the trip, Effie's heart ached for him, but she said goodbye and managed to hide her tears. As he was about to leave, Erny turned to her and said, 'This will be my last trip.'

Erny had been gone for some weeks when Effie had her last wisdom tooth extracted by a visiting dentist. She suffered dreadfully during the extraction, and for weeks afterwards could get no relief from the pain. Effie became so bad that the doctor at the AIM hospital sent word to Erny to leave his camels and come home by the first car he could find. It was the first time in nine years of Erny travelling with his camels that he had been brought home because of her health and Effie felt very bad about it. But with Erny's return, a great load rolled off Effie's shoulders.

The pain continued unabated, however, and six weeks after the initial extraction the AIM doctor gave Effie a whiff of ether and opened up her gum, removing considerable pus and splinters of bone. After this, the trouble gradually cleared up, but it was another pointer along the way of their need to return to an easier life down south.

Asking the Lord to guide their steps, Erny sent a message out to Mr Chapman regarding buying the property, but for several weeks there was no response. Erny spent the time tidying up the garden while they waited. Then suddenly, they received an acceptable offer from Mr Chapman. Erny sent a wire to the mission secretary who, with no prospective missionaries to replace them, advised Erny to accept Mr Chapman's offer.

Yet when they tried to contact Mr Chapman on the Friday they were told he was 350 miles (560km) from Alice Springs and there was no way to reach him. So they decided to continue on with the work there until such time as the Lord saw fit to make the way clear to them.

On the Saturday night Erny and Effie had a time of prayer. They poured out their hearts to God, recalling all the ways he had led and provided for them in the past. Then Sunday morning, on the way back from taking Sunday School, Erny met Mr Chapman in the street. He was in town on another matter and gladly lunched with them. But being Sunday, Erny would not enter into any business arrangements that day. Monday morning, the 17th September 1934, the papers were signed and the die was cast.

That night, as Erny and Effie knelt together in prayer, the reality hit them and the tears flowed. However, they realised it was for the best, and they set their hearts to discover what God had in store for them in the years to come.

Soon after they were married Erny had mentioned to Effie that one day he would like to take her to Switzerland to meet his family, but there had never been any surplus funds to make this possible. Now, with the sale of their property, Erny felt that, as some of the money for the house had come from his family, he was justified in using part of the proceeds to take Effie on a visit to Switzerland.

Earlier on Effie's eldest sister, Flora, had said she would gladly have the girls stay with her if ever Erny and Effie had the chance of a holiday. Now Effie wrote to Flora to see if this offer still stood. It was confirmed by return mail, and everything seemed to be falling into place.

But Erny and Effie knew they couldn't leave without paying a quick farewell visit to their long-time friends, Friederich and Minna Albrecht and family, along with all their other friends at Hermannsburg. Erny, Effie and the girls spent two pleasant yet sad days there. On the last evening they were given a special farewell, where Pastor Albrecht spoke movingly about their work together and how they would all miss them. Blind Moses spoke touchingly of meeting Erny and Effie on their first visit to Hermannsburg fourteen years earlier, and what their continued friendship in the Lord had meant to him. Other Aboriginal people followed, and as each one shared their memories, the tears flowed freely.

When Erny and Effie returned to Alice Springs they found Miriam had injured her back and could hardly move. They prayed for her and she managed to come over for prayer and Bible reading the next morning, even though they could see she was still in a lot of pain. However, the following morning she came in all smiles and said Teddy had something to tell them. He cheerfully related the following story.

The previous night he had been lying awake asking God to heal Miriam when suddenly, through the open doorway, he saw a bright light coming towards their little hut. It stopped right by their door and was so beautiful it lit up everything inside. Teddy suddenly realised it must be Jesus coming to heal Miriam. He awakened her and, as she looked towards the light, her back was completely healed and she never had another moment's pain from it.

Erny and Effie thought this was a marvellous confirmation to them that, although they were going away, the Lord would still be with his Aboriginal children, and would care for them in sickness and in trouble. As they shared these thoughts with Teddy and Miriam the four of them rejoiced together in the wonder of God's love and care for them all.

On their final Sunday morning in Alice Springs Erny drove the family out to a Aboriginal camp not far from town, where Faith played the portable organ and Erny preached his last sermon to them. While helping at the Melbourne mission twelve years previously, Erny's finger had been crushed in a printing press. It had healed with the end joint stiff, and he'd had to be careful over the years not to get it caught in anything. But this Sunday, while cranking the engine after the service, the crank handle backfired, seriously mangling Erny's stiff finger. They returned to Alice Springs as quickly as possible, where the doctor bandaged it temporarily for him.

That night Ebenezer Tabernacle was packed with Aborigines who had come from far and wide to farewell their beloved pastor and his family who had done so much for them over the years. Most of those present had come to know and love the Lord Jesus because of Erny's and Effie's ministry among them. In spite of an extremely painful finger, Erny sensed God's presence in their midst and preached his final sermon to them from a full heart. The following morning, under ether, the doctor removed the badly damaged joint.

The next day a young fellow came and offered Erny cash for his camel team. Everything, apart from Erny's finger, was coming together nicely. Yet, as Erny and Effie took one last walk around their property, there was a lump in their throats. The garden, which had taken so much effort to establish in the early years, was now flourishing with citrus trees, grape vines, date palms, almonds, pomegranates, olives, mulberries and various vegetables. When people had commented on their lush garden, Erny would explain, 'Erny sowed, Teddy watered and God gave the increase.'

Their little group of four goats had now grown into a large herd of between 200 and 300, with Aboriginal goat herders, including Mickey's wife, Rosie, caring for them. These goats had provided much needed milk, butter and meat over the years, and in a way, Erny and Effie felt they were abandoning them, although others would now benefit from the large herd.

They sold what furniture they could and gave some things away, but there was still a great deal to be sent by rail or taken south with them. One of their neighbours was also going south just then and readily took some of their extra luggage in his truck. Colin had recently finished his boiler-maker's course, and was marking time before moving to Victoria, so he was able to come up and help with the final packing. With Erny's finger still causing considerable trouble it was a real provision of the Lord, especially having Colin available to drive them down to Adelaide in the old car.

Just eight and a half months after the previous trip south with Mary they said their final farewells. Then, with decidedly mixed feelings, Erny and Effie sadly turned their backs on the only home they had known since they were married, more than twenty-two years earlier.

Chapter 20

AFTERWARDS

It took them eight days to drive the 981 miles (1571 km) to Adelaide with the engine continually overheating and various parts needing attention. This forced them to make a number of stops at stations along the way, where those who had known Colin as a small boy happily renewed their acquaintance.

Eventually, they arrived safely in Adelaide and Erny went immediately to see his good friend, Doctor Charles Duguid, about his agonising finger. At the Memorial Hospital Doctor Duguid removed a second joint that had now become gangrenous and referred Erny to an orthopaedic surgeon in Melbourne for follow-up treatment.

The family finally reached Gippsland in time for a happy Christmas reunion with Effie's father and youngest sister, Emily, and her husband. Before long Mary had to return to Bible College, and Colin secured a new position and lodgings at Heidleburg, 10 miles (16 km) from Melbourne.

Then, after leaving eleven year old Faith and eight year old Grace with Effie's sister, Flora, on the 5th March 1935 Erny and Effie finally set off on the Italian liner, *Romolo* for their long awaited trip to Switzerland. The refreshing sea voyage was followed by a most enjoyable time visiting Erny's family in Basle, Switzerland, whom he had not seen for more than twenty years. Yet as Erny excitedly introduced Effie to the majestic, snow-capped mountains of his homeland, she couldn't help contrasting their pristine beauty with the flat, heat-filled, red-dust gibber plains of their years in Central Australia.

Leaving Switzerland, Erny and Effie spent a few days in Germany, visiting family as well as the late Pastor Carl Strehlow's wife, Frieda. On Effie's first trip to Alice Springs, Frieda Strehlow had been a real mother to her and now Frieda was thrilled that Erny and Effie had taken the time to come and visit her.

From Germany they travelled on to London where, on the 3rd of June, Erny spoke at a Bible Society meeting. Then it was on to Scotland to visit Effie's relatives, most of whom she had never met. Their happy time here, however, was interrupted by the sad news that Effie's father had gone to be with his Lord. Even in the midst of their grief, though, they were able to thank God for the happy memories of their last Christmas together.

On the 24th October Erny and Effie arrived back in Melbourne, grateful for a wonderful holiday, yet with a prayer in their hearts that God would now make His will clear regarding their future service for Him.

They were able to buy a comfortable weatherboard home at Northcote, about 7 miles (11km) from Melbourne, where the family were happy to be together once more after so many years of separation. Before long, Erny, Effie, Colin and Mary became active members of the thriving Northcote Baptist Church, with Faith and Grace happily involved in Sunday School, Christian Endeavour and Youth Group activities.

Erny was appointed local representative of the British and Foreign Bible Society, with Effie serving on the Ladies' Auxiliary. For the next fifteen years Erny travelled throughout Victoria speaking to people of all denominations about the work of the Bible Society. Years afterward, people still remembered the cheerful Swiss Bible Society representative who yodelled his way into their hearts.

Throughout these years, Erny continued to share the needs of the outback with congregations and individuals whenever the opportunity arose. He also took services and showed slides to Aborigines at the Framlingham settlement. In time, Erny became Vice President of the Aborigines Uplift Society. One of his projects in this role involved approaching governments and businessmen alike in an effort to purchase cement to line and secure various outback waterholes frequented by the Aborigines.

Drought was a constant problem in the outback. At Hermannsburg water had to be carted by camel from Kaporilya Springs, 4.5 miles (7km) away. In 1935 Jeannie Gun donated autographed copies of her book, *We of the Never Never,* to help raise funds for a pipeline to provide continuous fresh water from the Springs for the Hermannsburg Mission. Erny rejoiced with his friends at the huge difference this made to the well-being of whites and Indigenous people alike.

Along with their continuing work on behalf of the Bible Society and Aborigines, Erny and Effie's lives were still deeply entwined with those of their children. In 1940 Colin moved to Adelaide and his cheerful company was greatly missed. However, three years later the family joyfully travelled to Adelaide to share in his marriage to long-time sweetheart, Phyllis, sister of Reverend Arthur Bottrell. Then, on the 15th October, 1947, Erny and Effie proudly welcomed their first grandchild, John Alexander Kramer. In 1969 John married Lesley Trigg and on the 3rd April 1971, their twin sons, Samuel and Benjamin, were born in Darwin.

Mary spent several happy years at the Melbourne Bible Institute. Following this she worked as a sister at the Melbourne City Mission and was also much involved in the Young Peoples' Christian Endeavour group at Northcote.

Grace was also very active in the Northcote church and was baptised there by Reverend Hansen. She began working in a bank, but later took up podiatry. In 1949 Grace transferred to Adelaide where she set up her own business and was greatly loved by all her clients for her kindness and gentleness. Erny and Effie had moved to Adelaide by the time 26 year old Grace married Douglas Dawson in 1951. Erny and Effie's second grandson, Robert Graeme Dawson, was born on the 9th February 1953.

Faith was also baptised by Reverend Hansen and later went into nursing, specialising in hospital theatre work. She spent fifteen years as matron of two Adelaide hospitals, nine of them at Wakefield Street Hospital. Then in December 1971, at the age of 49, Faith went to Zambia, Central Africa, where she spent five years as a medical missionary with the Australian Baptist Missionary Society. This was followed by a further nine years in Papua New Guinea teaching nurses at the Tinsley Health Centre, Baiyer River, along with trekking or flying to villages with the Missionary Aviation Fellowship. Faith returned to PNG three times after her 60th birthday, followed by another year helping out in Zambia during an emergency there.

The retiring age in Victoria was sixty, therefore in 1950 Erny and Effie, along with Mary, moved to Adelaide where the retiring age was 65, so that Erny could continue deputising for the Bible Society. They soon became active members of the Mitcham Baptist Church. With help from Colin, Erny subcontracted and built a home in Torrens Park (now Lower Mitcham). As with their church in Alice Springs, they called their new home 'EBENEZER', from 1 Samuel 7:12, 'Hitherto has the Lord helped us'.

After serving with the Bible Society for more than forty years, half of it in Australia's harsh outback, Erny finally retired in December 1954 at the age of 65. In February 1958 he was diagnosed with acute leukemia and passed to his eternal reward a short time later at the age of 68. His funeral was conducted by the minister of the Flinders Street Baptist Church, Reverend Leslie Gomm.

At the news of Erny's death, Professor Cleland wrote to Effie,

'On behalf of the Board for Anthropological Research of the University, and personally, may I convey to you and your family our deepest sympathy. The Board owed a great deal of the success of several of its expeditions to the great help given to it by Mr Kramer, whose knowledge of the Aborigines was of the greatest service. I think that much of this success was due to the Christian influences following on his ministrations to the Aborigines so that they had the utmost confidence in him. His life was one well spent on behalf of others. Yours sincerely, John Cleland.'

As daughter Mary said, 'Dad was most ingenious with his many "firsts" in Alice Springs, but he was a very humble man who would rather be remembered as the person who pointed his indigenous friends to their Lord and Saviour, the Lord Jesus Christ, and who praised God that many accepted Him and their lifestyles were completely changed to a new way of life. To God, Erny would give ALL the glory.'

Effie continued serving the Lord faithfully until failing health took its toll. On the 20th August, 1971, in her 85th year, Effie Kramer passed into the presence of her Lord and was reunited with her beloved Erny. Her funeral was conducted by the Reverend Leslie Gomm, assisted by Reverend Neil Adcock, with Reverend G Morling of New South Wales speaking at the graveside.

A small woman of only 4ft 9inches (145cm), Effie had a deep love for her Saviour and a tenacity of purpose that carried her through the almost overwhelming difficulties and hardships she encountered during her years of service for her Lord. We can well imagine the Master's words in Matthew 25:23 being spoken to both Erny and Effie, 'Well done, good and faithful servants ... Enter into the joy of your Lord.'

* * * * *

Postscript : Grace died in 1984 aged 58 and Colin in 1999 aged 86. On the 3rd June, 2000, Faith married Harold Metters. Mary then moved into a unit at All Hallows, and Ebenezer, the family's home for fifty years, was finally sold. In 2006 Mary passed into the presence of her Lord at the age of 88.

GOVERNMENT HOUSE
ADELAIDE
SOUTH AUSTRALIA

6th April, 1977.

Dear Miss Kramer,

Both Lady Nicholls and I were delighted to receive your letter of the 27th March, 1977, giving us news about the new Church at Alice Springs to be named the Kramer Memorial Church.

Your Father's name was widely respected for the great work he did as a missionary and we are delighted to know that his successor has seen fit to arrange for this new Church to be dedicated in memory of your Father.

I know that your Father would have been delighted to know that somebody is following in his footsteps with the worthwhile work that he was pleased to do.

I send my greetings and best wishes to all associated with the Kramer Memorial Church.

Yours sincerely,

Nicholls

GOVERNOR.

Miss Mary C. Kramer,
C/O Territory Motel,
Leichhardt Terrace,
ALICE SPRINGS.
S.A. 5750

AA 669 Ernest Eugene and Euphemia Kramer

Guide to Records

HOME
PROVENANCE
SERIES LIST
INDEX

About the Records

How to use this Finding Aid

Archival Terms

Provenance

Series List and Summary Descriptions

Inventory Listing by Series

Series AA669/01 – Ernest Eugene Kramer expedition and travel diaries

Series AA669/02 – Ernest E Kramer's notebooks primarily relating to the study of Aranda [Arrernte] language

Series AA669/03 – Euphemia Kramer's travel diaries

Series AA669/04 – Ernest E Kramer's letterbook

Series AA669/05 – Publications relating to Ernest E Kramer's work and other mission work among Aboriginal people in Australia

Series AA669/06 – Papers, correspondence and photographs relating to Central Australia and the Kramer family

Series AA669/07 – Negatives of Ernest E Kramer's missionary van

Index

Tindale's Catalogue of Australian Aboriginal Tribes

These records are managed by the **South Australian Museum**.
All queries relating to access should be made to the **Archives Access Officer**.

Published by the SOUTH AUSTRALIAN MUSEUM ARCHIVES
on the South Australian Museum website, 2004
Listed by Mandy Paul
HTML edition
Updated 2 February 2008
http://www.samuseum.australia.sa.com/aa669/index.html

The template for this Finding Aid is part of the
Heritage Documentation Management System

[TOP OF PAGE | HOME | SERIES | PROVENANCE | INDEX]

AA 669 Ernest Eugene and Euphemia Kramer Guide to Records

Series AA669/05

HOME
PROVENANCE
SERIES LIST
INDEX

Publications relating to Ernest E Kramer's work and other mission work among Aboriginal people in Australia

Date Range	1925? - 1978, four of the six items are undated.
Quantity	1.5 cm. 6 - 2 pamphlets, 2 booklets, 1 book, 1 magazine
Provenance	Ernest Eugene & Euphemia Kramer
Description	This series comprises six items: two pamphlets, two booklets, a book and a magazine. One leaflet and one booklet relate directly to the work of Ernest E Kramer, and one booklet to the Aborigines' Friends' Association (see AA 1).

Inventory Listing

AA 669/5/1-6 Publications relating to Ernest E Kramer's work and other mission work among Aboriginal people in Australia
This series includes the following items:

1. 'Australian Caravan Mission to Bush People and Aboriginals: Journeyings in the Far North and Centre of Australia.' By Ernest E Kramer. Undated 30 page booklet, illustrated with photographs, which includes references to travels through the Flinders Ranges and mission work in Oodnadatta.

2. 'The Ebenezer Tabernacle First Church Building in Alice Springs.' Undated 4 page pamphlet, with photograph of Ernest E Kramer's 'native helper' Micky Dow-Dow outside the church on front. Published by the Australian Missionary Society, Alice Springs.

3. *Australian Aborigines. Photographs.* Undated 64 page booklet published by the Aborigines' Friends' Association (see AA 1). Includes many photographs with captions, also the objectives of the AFA, a foreword, and 'An Aboriginal Pleads for His Race' by David Unaipon.

4. 'Native Women are Slaves.' Undated 16 page pamphlet by Andrew J Pearce, of the United Aborigines Mission, Finniss Springs, SA. Published by S John Bacon, Melbourne.

5. *Blackfellows of Australia.* By Charles Barrett & AS Kenyon. A Sun Book. Undated, 44 pages.

6. *On Being: The Bible: How has the Infallibe [sic] God spoken?* August 1978, 62 page magazine. Hawthorn.

This series contains references to the following regions of South Australia: North Central; Flinders Ranges.

This series contains references to: Northern Territory.

Creator Ernest Eugene & Euphemia Kramer
Control AA 669/5/1-6
Date Range 1925? - 1978, Four of the six items are undated.
Quantity 1.5 cm, 1 Albox album
Formats Ephemera
Inventory Identifier AA 669/5/1-6
Series AA669/05

www.ingramcontent.com/pod-product-compliance
Lightning Source LLC
LaVergne TN
LVHW051136080426
835510LV00018B/2438